HELP THEM THRIVE

LEADERSHIP COACHING FOR HUMANS LEADING HUMANS

MELISSA MAJORS

Help Them Thrive: Coaching for Humans Leading Humans

Melissa Majors

MELISSA MAJORS
CONSULTING

Copyright© 2024 by Melissa Majors Consulting

Published by Melissa Majors Consulting, melissamajors.com

Photo Credits: Adobe

ISBN: 979-8-218-36242-3

All rights reserved. No part of this publication may be reproduced, distributed, or transmitted in any form or by any means, including photocopying, recording, or other electronic or mechanical methods, without the prior written permission of the publisher, except in the case of brief quotations embodied in critical reviews and certain other noncommercial uses permitted by copyright law.

Limit of Liability/Disclaimer of Warranty: While the publisher and author have used their best efforts in preparing this book, they make no representations or warranties concerning the accuracy or completeness of the contents of this book and expressly disclaim any implied warranties of merchantability or fitness for a particular purpose. No warranty may be created or extended by sales representatives or written sales materials. The advice and strategies contained herein may not be suitable for your situation. You should consult with a professional where appropriate. Neither the publisher nor the author shall be liable for any loss of profit or any other commercial damages, including but not limited to special, incidental, consequential, or other damages.

Readers should be aware that Internet Web sites offered as citations and/or sources for further information may have changed or disappeared between the time this was written and when it is read.

I dedicate this book to my favorite adventurers, Shawn and Ashleigh.
You've chosen to thrive and live a more fulfilled life.
You are an inspiration to us all.

TABLE OF CONTENTS

Welcome	7
Chapter 1: Unintentionally Toxic	13
Chapter 2: Fair Leadership	25
Chapter 3: Well Being	37
Chapter 4: Pesky Emotions	63
Chapter 5: Confusing Feedback	85
Chapter 6: Declutter The Workload	95
Chapter 7: Humans Need Friends	103
Chapter 8: The Next Steps	117
Acknowledgments	123
About The Author	129

WELCOME

This isn't your typical leadership book; it's a discussion between you and me — human leaders who want to become even better leaders of other humans and ourselves. I'm Melissa Majors, your friend — with coaching benefits. I'm thrilled you decided to read this book. It's written like a conversation we would have as if we were chatting in a one-on-one coaching session. As your coach, I share performance-accelerating tactics on how to embrace our humanity and detoxify unintentionally toxic workplaces. As your friend, I coach with compassion, understanding, and encouragement, not shame or judgment for yourself or your colleagues.

Help Them Thrive

My guidance is based on 20+ years of practical experience leading and coaching happy and high-performing diverse groups of humans, some of my favorite leadership experts, and relevant data from a few of the world's leading research firms. Blend that with my unfair advantage as a coach, shaped by countless learning experiences I've developed throughout my career as a learning and development leader. I know how to close the gap between actual and desired performance.

I humbly acknowledge that helping others thrive and unlock their potential is a natural gift I possess — for which I am deeply grateful. Let me be clear: I do not have all the answers to every leadership challenge you face. I am not omniscient; I'm only human—a human who knows how to lead humans and bring the best out in them.

Throughout this discussion, I'll lead you on a journey to discover solutions from within your mind and perspective. That's what great coaches do. They don't spoon-feed you the answers; they help you reflect on how you think, feel, and behave. As your coach, I'll set the context with relatable stories and data, then ask well-placed questions that spark introspection and action.

My style is intentionally non-threatening. So please feel completely safe on this journey of enlightenment and growth. We can talk about hard stuff without making the conversation hard.

Welcome

Get ready for a lighthearted, non-judgmental, yet relevant and actionable discussion. Change is hard enough, so let's have fun while doing it!

We read global reports about engagement and leadership trends, but do we see ourselves in the results? Most of us tend to believe that the data applies to someone else and think, "I'm not who they're talking about." Introspection is hard. Psychologist Jeremy Dean, PhD, founder and author of PsyBlog, says,

> "Modern psychologists have discovered that the stories we weave about our mental processes are logically appealing but fatally flawed more often than we'd like to think. The gulf between how we think our minds work, as accessed through introspection, and how they actually work is sometimes so huge it's laughable."

Friend, as we mindfully examine our leadership impact, we'll likely recognize situations and behaviors that led to unintentionally toxic workplaces. Please do not shame yourself as you deepen your awareness. Instead, note the contrast between what you did versus what you'll do differently in the future.

I've learned much more from my failures than my successes. Let's choose to gain wisdom from our missteps rather than shame ourselves. Let's be grateful for self-awareness as it informs and motivates us to become even better leaders.

If we remain unaware, we can't improve. Self-awareness is a gift; embrace it without shame.

Throughout this book, I'll prompt you to journal your thoughts. I encourage you to pause, ponder, and answer the questions. Doing so will improve comprehension and increase the likelihood that you'll remember and apply your new-found knowledge when needed. Sure, you can simply read the book and then stick it on a shelf, but you risk forgetting profound insights and capitalizing on your motivation to try things differently. You have too much potential not to tap into your own wisdom, friend.

Perhaps you're also willing to share your thoughts with me? I'd love to hear from you! I've included QR codes to connect us and some that lead you to resources that I've curated.

This book is intentionally short and sweet. Human leaders don't have time for over-engineered, complex solutions to leadership. We need simple advice we understand and can use. And with that, let's begin.

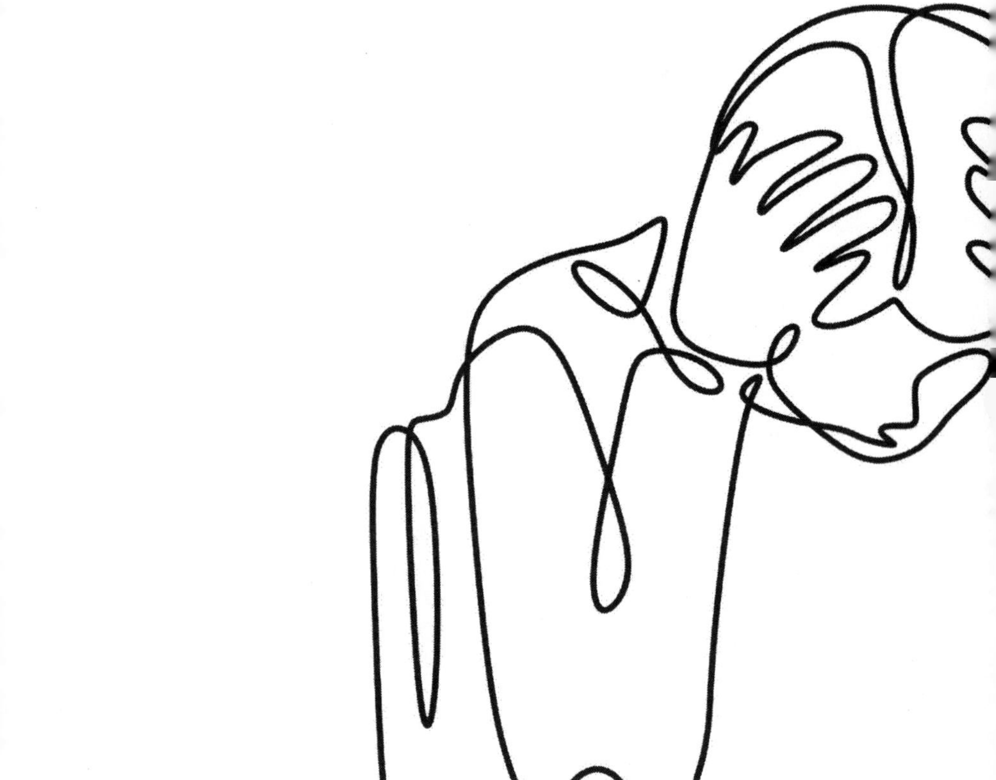

Chapter 1
UNINTENTIONALLY TOXIC

Are you familiar with the term Memento Mori? It's essentially a Latin concept that means, "Remember, you must die." You're likely thinking, "Oh great, this book is starting on a morbid note." Let me explain. Memento Mori reminds us that life is precious yet fleeting. Reflecting on our mortality encourages us to be more intentional about living a fulfilled life while we still can.

I have two sons – Terrance and Luke. When they were about four and five years old, Terrance took a nasty fall on some roller skates and hit the pavement flat on his back. Boom! The wind got knocked out of him, and he just lay there motionless.

Meanwhile, Luke approaches, stands over his brother's body, and casually asks, while continuing to munch on his snack, "Is he dead?" My mouth fell open with shock from his apathetic behavior, and I exclaimed, "Why would you ask a question like that?" Luke looked at me and said matter-of-factly, "Mommy, dead is not bad; it's just dead."

Out of the mouths of babes...come some peculiar yet thought-provoking perspectives.

I tell you that story to illustrate that Memento Mori acknowledges that death is simply part of the human condition. When pondered, we might discover the motivation and desire to cherish each day and strive to live a more fulfilled life.

> "Life is to be enjoyed, not endured."
> – Scott Peterson, MSgt, US Airforce Retired
> and My Beloved Uncle

A few years back, during the global pandemic, workers faced unfortunate and soul-shaking reminders of mortality. As a result, their intrinsic motivators shifted, and what success looked like had changed. Human workers became curious about their purpose and were inspired to live a more energy-balanced life. They stopped delaying their bucket list items, and many decided they

Unintentionally Toxic

didn't want to live to work; they wanted to work to live.

So, they decided to act on their newly found spirit of adventure. Many ran to their nearest adventure stores and bought campers, skis, boats, and other outdoor toys to venture into the fresh air untethered by the constraints of quarantined homes, commutes, and physical offices.

They became accustomed to taking walks, spending quality time with loved ones, and being more productive on work projects due to fewer distractions and interruptions. They saved money on gas, dry cleaning, lunch expenses, etc. Many experienced a better, more balanced life, albeit amid tragedy.

Workers realized that their jobs were sucking the life out of them. They preferred the autonomy of choosing when, where, and how they worked. They contemplated their desired quality of life compared to reality and decided their job wasn't worth the cost of an unfulfilled life.

This enlightenment prompted workers to analyze the lopsided ratio of energy spent on work versus life, so over 50 million Americans quickly became disenchanted. They went to their bosses, channeled their inner Johnny

Paycheck, and said, *"Take this job and shove it; I ain't working here, no more'!"* For those who haven't heard that song yet, you must listen. Scan this QR code to enjoy!

15

Help Them Thrive

"The Great Resignation" has been widely discussed, so we won't belabor it here. However, the leadership lesson we must learn from this mass exodus is that humans want to live better lives and now know first-hand what it's like. They finally experienced the tangibleness of work-life balance. The pandemic was tragic and stressful on so many levels; however, it had its silver linings, and learning to be mindful and rebalance the energy we spend on work and life was undoubtedly one of them.

At the end of our lives, no one says, "I wish I had worked more." All we can hope for is the people we love will love us in return. Memento mori, friend.

As leaders of humans, we have the privilege of modeling what good leadership looks like to those we influence. So, how are you doing? Are you thriving? Is your team thriving?

Self

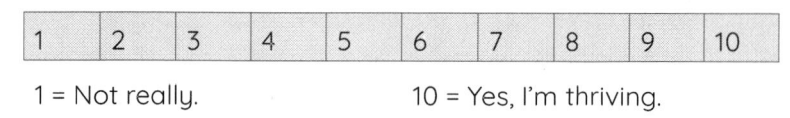

1	2	3	4	5	6	7	8	9	10

1 = Not really.　　　　　10 = Yes, I'm thriving.

Team

1	2	3	4	5	6	7	8	9	10

1 = Not really.　　　　　10 = Yes, they are thriving.

According to Gallup's 2023 State of the Global Workplace Report, Gallup estimates that low engagement costs the global economy $8.8 trillion, which happens to be 9% of the global GDP. Yikes! That's enough to make the difference between success and failure for humanity.

In the United States.

- Only 31% of people report thriving at work.
- 52% are not engaged or relatively quiet quitting.
- 17% are loud quitting.

We probably agree that those results are dismal. But what do we do about it? And should we care about engagement, well-being, and retention as much as we care about bottom-line metrics like profitability, expense, and revenue? What often happens is during a leadership meeting, an HR representative reports data on employee engagement, satisfaction, and retention. We react with celebration or shock, then quickly move on to higher prioritized discussions, like the financial results.

Imagine with me that we are sitting on the most beautiful beach you've ever seen; close your eyes and visualize warm white sand, the sound of the tide, and seagulls flying above. There are no sharp rocks or icky algae, pollution, bottle caps, or anything that would deter you from thriving at this beautiful beach. Would you like to go hang out in this paradise with me? I'm in; let's do it! We would have such a wonderful time. We'll channel our inner Zac Brown Band and sing the lyrics from the song Toes.

We'll "Have our toes in the water, ass in the sand, not a worry in the world, and a cold beer in our hand; life is good today...life is good today."

Picture us sitting there on the edge of the water, eating ceviche, drinking margaritas, and having the time of our lives. Life would be good indeed.

Then, all of a sudden, a wave catches us off guard and washes up to where we're sitting. We scurry about, trying to catch our trash as the wave drags our cups, napkins, and bottles into the sea.

We **unintentionally** pollute the water.

Say the word **unintentional** out loud. So often, we, as leaders, unintentionally pollute our work environments. We don't intend for it to happen, but it happens, nonetheless.

Imagine our team members go to hang out at that same beach after we've been there. They enter the water expecting the same lovely experience we had. But instead of thriving, they start bumping into our unintentional trash. What do you think they would do? What would you do? They would get out of the water. Yuck. Who wants to swim in a polluted environment?

Friend, this scenario is an analogy for our workplaces. As leaders, we often unintentionally pollute the environment, causing our teams to disengage, quit, or keep swimming but loathe every minute.

No leader wakes up and says, "I want my team to fail today!" Yet here we are. More humans are failing at work than thriving. It happens because unintentional pollutants have inadvertently toxified our work environments.

Humans don't thrive in toxic environments.

MIT Sloan management review studied The Great Resignation to determine what was truly causing people to leave our organizations in droves. What they discovered is that compared to salary, workers are ten times more likely to quit if they believe the culture is toxic.

They dug deeper to define the attributes of a healthy versus toxic environment and discovered that a healthy workplace has four characteristics:

- Workers are treated fairly.
- They feel like they belong and are welcome to be there.
- They are included in key decisions.
- Diverse groups of employees are represented.

Seems simple enough, right? Most of us believe we are already doing many of these things; however, based on these data, there is clearly a disconnect between our perceived versus real leadership impact.

Help Them Thrive

Gallup reports that the manager or team leader alone accounts for 70% of the variance in team engagement.

So, friend, the most significant lever we can pull to improve team engagement and detoxify our workplaces is to become even better leaders so the humans we influence can thrive. When employees thrive, they take better care of the end customer. When end customers thrive, they take care of our bottom line. Employee engagement and well-being aren't some squishy metrics that only HR should care about. There is a direct correlation between the quality of the employee experience and the financial health of our companies.

But let's be honest: talking about numbers is easier than talking about humans. Humans are far more complicated. Or are the needs of human workers simpler and more straightforward than we realize? Perhaps we're operating in such a fast-paced, complex time that we overengineer solutions and unintentionally ignore human's basic needs.

Let's examine some tactics related to creating a healthy work environment. Please answer the following questions.

Unintentionally Toxic

Overall, how healthy or toxic (based on the criteria we discussed) is your work environment?

1	2	3	4	5	6	7	8	9	10

1 = Toxic   10 = Healthy

Now, think about the three best leaders you've ever worked with or know. Who are they?

_____

_____

_____

_____

Describe the tactics they've used to treat others fairly.

_____

_____

_____

_____

List examples of their actions that make colleagues feel welcome and have a sense of belonging at work.

_____

_____

_____

_____

Describe how they intentionally included lower-ranking colleagues in key decisions, especially the ones that affect those same people.

Considering the behavior of the leaders you describe, list one or two of their tactics that you could also use to help your team thrive.

Tactic Number 1:

Tactic Number 2:

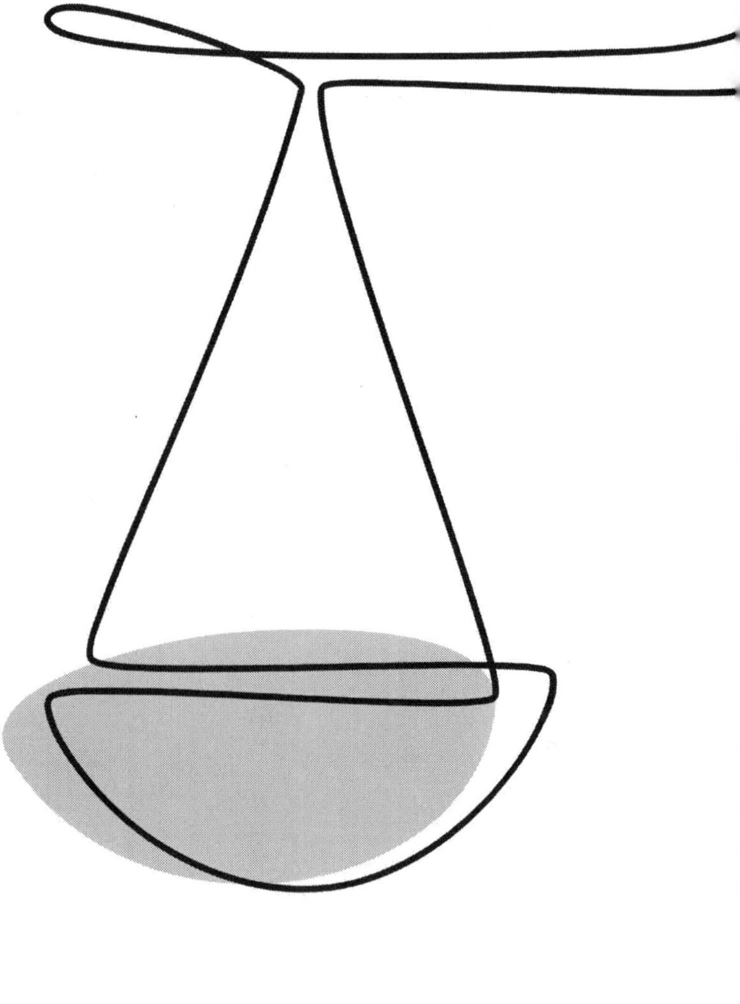

CHAPTER 2
FAIR LEADERSHIP

Have you ever witnessed or heard a colleague say they were being mistreated? Based on my research, 95% of people answer "Yes" to this question. This means that most of us have observed people being mistreated at work.

Because it's such a common occurrence, have we unintentionally normalized unfair treatment as a typical condition of employment experience? When you witnessed the mistreatment of others, what did you do about it? Here's what usually happens: we unintentionally overlook their perspective instead of truly understanding and empathizing with their experience.

This unintentional ignoring can sound like...

"Oh, she's a great person. I'm sure she didn't mean to offend you."

"You're being too sensitive. It was just a joke."

"That's just how he is. He treats everybody the same way, so don't take it personally."

Do those phrases sound familiar? We commonly, yet unintentionally, dismiss the offended's perspective much more than we realize. This may not seem like a big deal. However, these experiences create feelings of unfairness and exclusion, which wreck their sense of belonging and safety.

As humans, we need to feel understood and accepted as much as we need to eat. It is just that vital to our ability to thrive. In my first book, The 7 Simple Habits of Inclusive Leaders, I describe Matthew Leiberman's research on how Maslow's Human Hierarchy of Needs got it partially right. In addition to food, shelter, and water, humans need to belong to social groups. So, when people feel mistreated, and we dismiss their perspective, it makes them feel like an outcast, and they experience a perceived break in their connection to the social group.

What do you think we as humans do to cope with the feelings of social disconnection? Let's first examine what's happening in our brains when we're treated unfairly. We feel threatened, and our brains kick into the threat state of "fight, flight, or freeze" mode.

In the threat state, our brain's amygdala, an almond-shaped structure located deep in the brain's temporal lobe, activates this response. This response is an innate, automatic reaction that prepares our bodies to either defend ourselves or flee from danger. It triggers the release of stress hormones, such as cortisol and adrenaline, which increase our heart rate, blood pressure, and breathing rate.

At the same time, the amygdala communicates with the prefrontal cortex, the part of the brain responsible for decision-making and rational thinking. The prefrontal cortex tries to understand the situation and determine the best action. However, when feeling threatened, the amygdala's intense emotional response often overrides the prefrontal cortex, leading us to act impulsively rather than rationally.

Humans don't thrive in a state of threat; we're just focused on surviving.

Our threat-state responses can result in an array of illogical behaviors. Think of a time when you witnessed a colleague treated unfairly. Circle the threat-state actions that took place.

Fought Back

Resigned

Froze

Disengaged

Gossiped

Became Irrational

Retaliated with passive-aggressive behavior.

Became irritated

Lost confidence

Stopped contributing

Quiet Quit (Started doing the bare minimum.)

Assimilate (Started behaving like the offenders to be less different and fit in.)

Other: _____

What commonly happens is their colleagues misinterpret this irrational behavior as a performance problem or character flaw — especially when we don't genuinely consider the unfair treatment they experience that prompted the illogical behavior. In short, their temporary, natural human reaction to being in a threat state tarnishes their reputation. Let's break this down. They get mistreated, react, and then get punished by being labeled as a poor performer, while the crux of the

Fair Leadership

problem is likely attributed to toxic conditions that make it nearly impossible for humans to thrive.

Let me be clear, there are legitimate poor performers that should be coached up or coached out. However, given the dismal engagement scores in most workplaces, how much is unfair treatment a contributor to the subpar performance of human workers? From my vantage point, it's the leading, most influential workplace polluter. Unfair treatment, which is often subtle and difficult to detect, makes this pollutant especially challenging to identify... unless you're the one receiving it.

As humans, we need to be understood and accepted as much as we need to eat. When we feel like outcasts, we don't thrive.

How do we stop the normalization of people being unintentionally mistreated at work? We mitigate it with tactical empathy.

I am a huge fan of Chris Voss and rave about his tactics in my book The 7 Simple Habits of Inclusive Leaders.

If you've read it, you know all about tactical empathy. However, it's such a powerful concept that a refresher on it is time well spent.

Chris Voss is the author of a book called Never Split the Difference. If you haven't read his book yet, I highly recommend it. Chris was the lead hostage negotiator for the FBI for 25 years. Let's imagine the bad guys kidnap you on vacation. Chris would be the one they would send in to negotiate your way to safety, and he has the most brilliantly relevant definition of empathy because it's action-oriented - tactical empathy, which he affectionately refers to as "weapons-grade empathy." Powerful, right?

Chris's definition aligns perfectly with what we as leaders need to practice to empathize with others effectively.

*Tactical Empathy: Describes and demonstrates an understanding of the needs, interests, and perspectives of others **without necessarily agreeing**.*
I want to emphasize the last three words of that definition, "without necessarily agreeing." We don't have to agree to empathize. We simply need to understand their perspective and make them feel understood, not necessarily agree with them.

Empathy isn't sympathy, and understanding doesn't constitute agreement.

How long have you been in a position of power? For more than five years? If so, I have bad news for you, friend: power causes "dame bramage," I mean, brain damage. Ha! There is compelling research coming out of the University of California, Berkeley, related to how power affects our brain's ability to empathize with others.

Many of us are grappling with this often undetectable quandary when we undervalue power's influence on our behavior.

Dacher Keltner at UC Berkeley found that "Under the influence of power, leaders acted as if they had suffered a traumatic brain injury-- becoming more impulsive, less risk-aware, and, crucially, less adept at seeing things from other people's point of view."

Please humor me while I grossly oversimplify this compelling research. Essentially, what happens to us is as we ascend to leadership ranks, we depend on other people's positive perceptions of us, our performance, and our decisions to gain collaboration and support.

Once we have risen to the ranks within our organizations, we've essentially "arrived" and are less dependent upon other people's approval for success. This research suggests that our brains start to become numb to the perspective of others because we no longer need them as much to succeed in our roles. We don't listen as much, consider other opinions, involve them in decision-making, and make them feel welcome. Yikes! Aren't these all the attributes of a healthy work environment? Yet the longer we're in a position of power, our brains can become anesthetized to these considerations.

We're in a quandary of power indeed. No wonder leaders are accused of making decisions in a vacuum and of being disconnected from those affected; our brains get in the way! Given the case we've already discussed for mitigating unfair treatment, it's vital that we learn to identify and mitigate the adverse effects of power and our ability to empathize. Note that power is not a bad thing. How we use it makes all the difference.

> "In listening lies great power. Many are experts in speaking (while everyone hears), adept in analyzing in bits and pieces, very prompt in commenting, and always ready to stamp judgment of 'right' or 'wrong'. Very few are skilled in listening, first, with the ears and then, with the heart.
>
> Those who do hold true,
> sustainable, and great power."
> **— Ufuoma Apoki**

How do the adverse effects of power show up at work? Think of a leader you respect who is under power's influence but likely doesn't realize it. Describe the unintentional ways in which they power over others and diminish their colleague's ability to thrive.

Thriving teams have leaders who practice empathy as a skill. It helps mitigate the quandary of power, uncovers vital insights, and makes others feel valued and seen. These leaders work hard at understanding others' perspectives, especially the ones they disagree with. Friend, most leaders are not empaths gifted with the natural ability to identify with the emotions, thoughts, or attitudes of others. Thriving leaders intentionally practice it as a skill to build competence.

If you aren't naturally empathetic, that's OK; it just means you must invest a bit more energy to build your empathy muscle. All things worth doing require practice, and empathy is one of the most important skills we, as leaders of humans, should hone.

I have a tactical empathy brain hack to bolster your practice. The next time you hear someone say they are being treated unfairly, I encourage you to follow these steps:

Step One: Listen deeply for understanding, not rebuttal. If you feel yourself getting defensive, your brain is moving into a threat state, which will prevent you from objectively understanding the other person. Remember, when in a threat state, our brains get illogical really quickly. Take a few deep, slow breaths. Doing so sends a signal to your brain that you're okay and don't need to prepare to defend against whatever they are saying.

Step Two: Thank them for opening up and sharing their perspective with you.

Step Three: Say something like, "Your experience here matters to me, and I want you to thrive. Let me repeat what you said to ensure I thoroughly understand."

Considering what we discussed so far, including this empathy hack, the power-influenced leader's behavior, and tactical empathy, what resonates most with you, and what will you do differently to become a more fair leader?

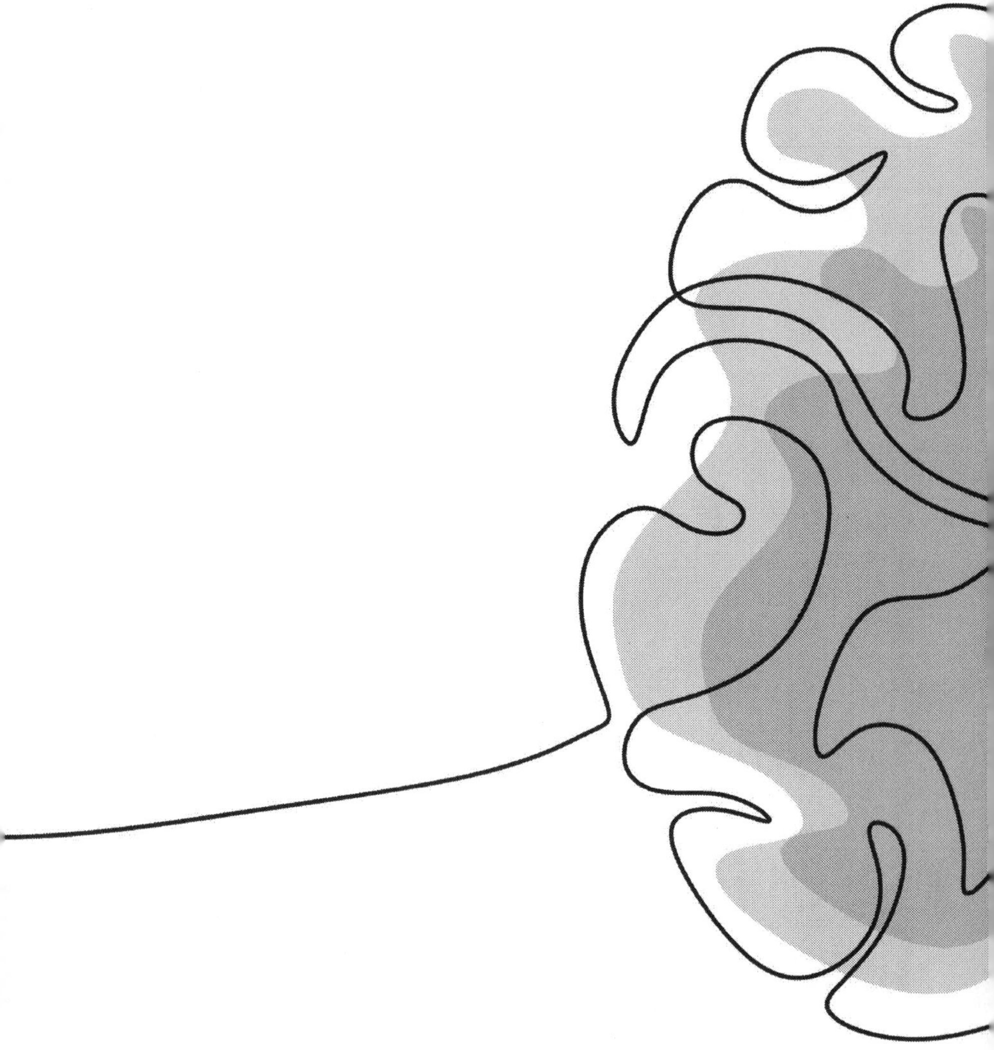

CHAPTER 3
WELL BEING

We cannot talk about helping workers thrive without prioritizing and discussing the importance of mental well-being and mitigating the adverse impacts of stress. As leaders, we must find a way to preserve our team's mental clarity and build resilience to stress. Let's be realistic in this exploration; stress is not going away.

The upside is that humans are designed to respond to acute stress. As you may recall, the threat state mechanism in our bodies and brains activates when we experience stress; our heart rate and blood sugar levels increase, which prepares us to run or fight and thus survive.

The downside is that humans aren't designed for the harmful effects of exposure to chronic stress. This ongoing exposure is significantly influencing human performance at work. It is wrecking our ability to think well, make sound decisions, collaborate, and engage.

Chronic stress at work can have detrimental effects on both our physical and mental well-being. Physically, it is associated with cardiovascular issues, weakened immune systems, and digestive problems. Mentally, it contributes to anxiety, depression, and burnout, impacting cognitive functions.

Work performance may decline with reduced productivity and increased absenteeism. Long-term risks include chronic diseases, and sleep patterns may be disrupted.

Humans don't thrive under chronic stress.

How many of you have experienced the dreaded "blue screen of death" on your computers? When this happens, your computer is basically saying, "Hi, I'm your computer. You've worked me too hard, and I'm done with you. I am shutting down. Better luck next time."

Argh! How did you react when you saw the blue screen of death? You were probably angry and beyond frustrated that it was happening. You likely lost files, emails, contact lists, etc. Yes, this is an incredibly inconvenient, frustrating, and stressful situation, but let's be honest:

Well Being

you knew the blue screen of death was coming before you saw it, didn't you?

Think about the signs and messages your screen was sending you before it flipped you the virtual bird. Hindsight is 20/20, but there are clear warning signs, friend. But like most busy humans, you likely ignored them. You might have heard a grinding or growling noise coming from your computer. Or it was slow to boot up. Perhaps it became glitchy and unpredictable.

Friend, the blue screen of death is an analogy for our brains. When burned out, our brains don't process well. We have difficulty comprehending information, making decisions, working well with others, and regulating emotions. We become cynical, irritable, and angry. When burned out, our brain essentially shuts down and becomes glitchy and dysfunctional, just like our computers do when overworked.

According to Deloitte's study on well-being, 52% of respondents report "always" or "often" feeling exhausted or stressed, and 43% report feeling overwhelmed. So, no wonder employees struggle to balance their energy because they are stressed out and overwhelmed to the point that they cannot perform well.

This same study discovered that only 56% of employees think their company's executives care about their well-being, while 91% of the C-suite think their employees believe they care. This vast gap in perspectives serves as compelling evidence of our lack of self-awareness as leaders.

As I mentioned, there's often a disconnect between what we *think* we do and what we *actually* do. We *think* we're creating workplaces where humans can thrive, but the reality is we aren't, and they don't think we care that they are struggling. Would you do your best work for a leader who doesn't seem like they care about your wellbeing? Probably not. You'd disengage if you're like the 69% of other global workers.

I burned myself out a few years ago. It was the year when my first book came out; it was a blessing and a curse. It was a blessing because it was well received, and my talks, coaching, and workshops were in high demand. I'm still humbled and honored that so many people were interested in meeting me and hearing what I had to say.

However, I was so elated with the demand that I neglected to create boundaries for myself. Within six months of the book launch, I racked up 75,000 air miles, all domestic travel within the US. One night here, one night there, one night here, one night there. By the end of the year, I was toast.

Here's how burnout affected me. I was in a perpetual state of "pissedoffedness." I snapped at my sweet children, barked at my patient husband, and was super quick to become angry. I'm usually very laid-back and happy, so this behavior was uncharacteristic. I wasn't sleeping well or motivated to exercise. I felt tired all the time. I was in a brain fog and couldn't think clearly, evidenced by the five times I would have to read an email before comprehending its message.

And since we're friends and adults, I don't mind sharing that when my husband would give me the googly eyes, I would react with, "Don't even think about touching me. Unless... you're going to rub my feet. Then we can probably work something out." My poor family caught the blues. And to make matters worse, I thought they were to blame for how I was feeling.

I was completely oblivious to the fact that I was burned out because I'm typically a very resilient person. I simply couldn't recognize what was happening to me. I felt guilty because I should have been feeling nothing but gratitude for the amazing success I had experienced and the support my family provided during the book writing and launch process.

Burnout affected me physically, mentally, and spiritually.

When most leaders ascend to the position of managing people, we also assume a typically unspoken expectation of higher performance, wisdom, and an overall sense that we have it all together. Ha!! Yeah...not so much. We're human, too, complete with all the demands and stressors of life, just like everyone else.

Help Them Thrive

We try our best, but oftentimes, we fall short, just like everyone else.

The difference is power. Because we have the authority to manage other people, expectations of us are higher. According to Microsoft's Work Trend Index — a global survey of workers across multiple industries and companies published in September 2022, managers are feeling burnout more than other workers, with a shocking 53 percent reporting burnout. According to the study, leaders have the highest levels of stress and the lowest levels of work-life balance in the workforce.

When stressed and burned out, we leak out on other people; you can't help it. You may think you're successfully covering for the fact that you are depleted, lost, and unfulfilled, but it shows. The quandary is that being the boss comes with perks, too - higher pay, more flexibility, status, and a sense of success. But those perks come with a cost, higher stress, and less empathy from others.

You've arrived; yippee and yikes!

Friend, we must learn to listen deeply and empathize with ourselves too. The constant grinding through chronic

Well Being

stress is not only burning us out, but we're also often burdened with feelings of guilt and shame.

A senior executive I coach said, "I don't have the right or the time to be burned out. Look at how much better I have it than others. What do I have to complain about?" Remember, what we *think* we do and what we *actually* do are not the same.

Burnout had transformed her from her team's best boss to an absolute tyrant. When we started working together, she genuinely couldn't understand why a mass exodus was occurring, let alone identify her role in the toxicity. Because she was the leader, she didn't feel she had the latitude to be vulnerable and acknowledge that she was spiraling. To her, and many, vulnerability is a sign of weakness. Friend, being vulnerable is a sign of humanness and courage.

Unaddressed burnout is like the aging process. You look in the mirror one day and become shocked to realize that you look different. "When did that happen?" Ha! It happens gradually, every day, like it does to all humans. Burnout has a sneaky way of transforming us into a different kind of leader, and typically not one that enables us to thrive.

Burned-out leaders don't thrive…and neither do the people around them.

Help Them Thrive

In Brene Brown's talk "Call to Courage" (Netflix) she said,

> *"It is so much easier to cause pain than feel pain, and people are taking their pain, and they're working it out on other people," she said, "and when you don't acknowledge your vulnerability, you work your shit out on other people. Stop working your shit out on other people."*

We typically don't intend to work our shit out on other people. It often happens because we lack self-awareness and don't even realize the devastation and stress we're creating for others. Being in pain should be a temporary state. But thanks to chronic stress, we risk transforming into a new and unimproved, burned-out version of ourselves.

When I was burned out, I didn't even realize I was in so much pain. The internal shaming associated with my privilege convinced me that I didn't have the right to acknowledge that I was suffering. You know the term, "Fake it 'til you make it?" In other words, pretend you don't have feelings and aren't vulnerable to burnout. Have we inadvertently become seduced into expecting workers to fake it and suppress their humanness to succeed at work? Are you giving yourself the latitude to be human and authentically act human at work? Or does the unreasonable expectation of, "Check your feelings at the door." still apply?

Well Being

Humans can't fake it 'til we make it. We fake it 'til we don't make it, burnout, disengage, or quit.

"Burnout" has become a popular catch-all term for anything that distresses people. Before we proceed with assessing your levels of burnout, let's define it based on The Maslach Burnout Inventory (MBI) a widely used psychological assessment tool designed to measure burnout in the workplace. It assesses burnout through three components: Emotional Exhaustion (feelings of emotional depletion), Depersonalization (negative attitudes toward work and colleagues), and Reduced Personal Accomplishment (perceived decline in competence and achievement).

Although the burnout label can be misused and misunderstood, it is an essential red-flag warning that indicates we're not thriving.

I must share that I'm grateful for burning out and recovering from it. Without that experience, I wouldn't have the insight and wisdom to mitigate it in the future. There are lessons in failure, friend, if we intentionally glean them. Once you know better, you can do better. So, let's talk about how we can recover from and prevent burnout.

One of the most effective ways to recover is to unplug from work, rest, and reset our mind, body, and spirit. Forbes published a must-read summary of enlightening research on burnout recovery conducted by Applied Psychology Health and Well-Being Journal.

You can read the full article by scanning this QR code.

Unplugging and resting is precisely what I did to rebound.

I went on a solo vacation and spent five days completely unplugged from life's stressors. I meditated, ate healthy foods, rested, enjoyed the spa, took strolls, and, most importantly, turned off my devices. The experience served as a reset for my mind, body, and spirit.

After only five days, I was recharged and thriving again. I recognize not everyone has the privilege and flexibility to unplug for a week; doing so was a treat and investment in my wellness that I will never regret or apologize for. I permitted myself to take a break, and it was precisely what I needed to be myself again.

Most workers are grinding through work in a chronic state of burnout. Imagine what that does to their performance. Imagine what it does to your perception of their capabilities. If they are operating in a state of burnout, they will be lower performers, and you, as leaders, will judge their performance negatively.

Burnout is a temporary state that can be remedied; it should not permanently reflect on human workers' performance as a character trait, yet we as leaders

Well Being

expect human workers to perform optimally and thrive even when burned out. Machines can't even do that, as evidenced by the blue screen of death analogy.

Humans don't thrive when burned out.

The concepts of state and trait in psychology distinguish between temporary and situational emotional conditions (state) influenced by external factors and enduring, stable characteristics (trait) that persist over time and across various situations, reflecting an individual's personality.

As leaders of ourselves and others, we cannot eliminate chronic stress. However, we can help ourselves and others build resilience and thwart some damaging effects on our minds, bodies, spirits, and performance.

I have a question: at what time of the day is your mind most clear? Circle your response below.

- Morning
- Afternoon
- Evening

If you're like 90% of most people, you chose morning. The brain generally functions more efficiently in the morning. You wake up, and your brain feels refreshed. I often hear people say their best ideas come to them during their morning showers, jogging, or other activities without distractions. Why is this?

Help Them Thrive

I'm not a neuroscientist, but a lover and student of the discipline. So, please humor this grossly oversimplified explanation of why we have brain clarity in the morning. Thanks to advances in neuroscience, we now know that stress on the brain is as damaging as smoking is to the lungs; no offense to smokers out there. I used to smoke when it was cool. I looked particularly sophisticated hanging out in Italy at cafés, drinking cappuccinos, and smoking cigarettes. It seemed cool and normal, but damaging, nonetheless.

Our brains release a chemical called cortisol when we're in stressful situations. As cortisol accumulates in our brains throughout the day, our thoughts become slower and less precise, which explains why it likely takes you much longer to read those late afternoon emails, comprehend what they mean, and even longer to reply intelligently. No wonder!

You're foggy because your brain's piping (neural pathways) is clogged from the cortisol buildup, and you become cognitively depleted. When you sleep, *if* you're sleeping well, you experience an REM (Rapid Eye Movement) cycle. This is a sleep phase where vivid dreaming occurs, and brain activity is high and comparable to wakefulness. REM sleep is crucial for memory consolidation, emotional regulation, and sleep quality.

Well Being

In short, during REM, it's like we have a brain-sweeping crew that comes in and cleans up our dirty little minds and clears out all that cortisol buildup. Please note this process only happens if you're sleeping well. If you aren't sleeping well, the gunk in your brain's pipelines accumulates, eventually leading to complete burnout or worse.

Prolonged exposure to elevated cortisol levels can damage the brain in various ways. This includes adverse impacts on cognitive functions, memory, and emotional regulation, as well as an increased risk of neurological disorders like Alzheimer's and dementia.

I was fortunate enough to participate in a workshop hosted by the Brain Performance Institute and gobbled up the wisdom of its founder, Sandra Bond Chapman, Ph.D., one of the nation's preeminent cognitive neuroscientists. Dr. Chapman and her team are conducting ground-breaking research on what makes the brain more robust, faster, and last longer.

Friend, there's hope for us yet! We can recover from burnout and improve our brain health to become even better thinkers than we are today.

Performance improves when our brain health improves.

During Dr. Chapman's workshop, she told the story of a squad of Navy Seals who were struggling with mental fog and cognitive fatigue. One soldier confided in her that he couldn't think clearly anymore and didn't trust himself to execute missions. For him, mistakes cost lives.

After following her simple advice for only four days, the soldiers regained their mental clarity and had the confidence to perform again. If it works for them, it will work for us.

Three Daily Steps to Help Our Brains Thrive

Step One: **Conduct at least three meaningful conversations.**

Dr. Chapman recommends conducting at least three meaningful conversations a day. You may think, "Melissa, I talk to people all day. I'm already doing this." You might talk to people, but are you having meaningful dialogues? Often, our conversations, especially those at work, are transactional.

"Did you get my email?"

"Did you send the invoice?"

"Was the payment received?"

"Did you schedule the meeting?"

"When is the project due?"

"What do you want for dinner?"

Transactional conversations aren't strenuous enough to exercise our brains. We are wired for social connection, so deep or meaningful conversations with other humans are like neuro workouts.

Psychologist Matthias Mehl and his team set out to study happiness and deep talk. Their research discovered that humans are driven to create meaning in their lives, which meaningful conversations do. Also, human beings are social animals who need to connect with others. If all we're having is small talk, we're neglecting a vital aspect of our biologically wired needs.

Step Two: **Think innovative thoughts seven times a day.** This may seem daunting, but I will give you some easy tips that don't take much time, which I'm sure you can incorporate.

You can ask yourself, "How can I do *x* differently?"

"What other route can I use to I drive to work?"

"How could I make this thing (process, product, conversation, hairstyle, etc.) even better?"

Pondering how to do something differently qualifies as an innovative thought and serves as an exercise for your brain. Let's practice it together. Write down three questions that will prompt you to think about how to do something differently.

Step Three: **Take five-minute brain breaks five times a day.**

You may think, "Melissa, I am running from meeting to meeting all day. I don't have time for lunch, let alone to take brain breaks five times a day!" I get it; you're legitimately busy.

The real question is, what's at stake if we don't do this? Are you satisfied with your team underperforming in the latter parts of the day, or do you want to preserve your team's best thinking, enable them to make smart decisions, and perform at peak levels? High-quality thinking and brain function are at stake here.

But I thoroughly understand the reality. Our days are so full of meetings that we logistically don't have time to take five-minute brain breaks. A brain break is being still, quiet, and breathing deeply. That's it. You can meditate on your own or use the help of guided meditation. I'm not talking about the type of meditation where you're sitting cross-legged, hum, and hold your fingers together. It's just a breathing break. Think of it like a smoke break but with clean air.

So, your team is too busy for brain breaks. I get it, but as leaders, we can solve the "I don't have time for brain breaks." objection. Create the space for them by conducting a brain break at the start of your meetings. Intimidated to lead a guided meditation? Yeah, me too. Good thing there is an app for that. At the start of meetings, especially ones that require innovative ideas or major decisions, I play a 3 to 5-minute guided meditation video. There are many excellent free and paid resources you can use. I'm particularly fond of Headspace.

Adding brain breaks to meeting agendas accomplishes a few goals. It conveys that you care enough about their well-being that you are willing to take time to collectively take a break. It also establishes an understanding that you prioritize stress reduction and mental clarity. Taking brain breaks demonstrates your humanness.

One of my coaching clients is a C-Suite leader for a Fortune 500 company. He recognized that his team was exhausted, overwhelmed, and approaching burnout. He'd thoroughly enjoyed the effects of the meditations we practiced in his coaching sessions, but he was reluctant to introduce them to his team without feeling unprofessional and weird.

He introduced the concept by saying, "This may feel a little awkward at first, but if your experience is like mine, you'll quickly find that these will help us build resilience to stress, boost our mental clarity, and make better decisions."

Notice how he proactively labeled the possibly uncomfortable feelings due to stigmas and skepticism that can be associated with meditation. After just the first brain break, his team noticed an immediate difference and wanted more. He witnessed an extreme increase in the quality of their conversations, ideas, and decisions. He also shared that they finished early in every meeting, which included a brain break. Finish meetings earlier? Yes, please!

Considering this discussion on well-being, which points resonate most, and what will you do differently as a result of this information?

_____

_____

_____

_____

_____

_____

_____

Creating boundaries to preserve well-being is vital to establishing a healthy balance between work and life.

Earlier in my career, I started a new job working for a terrific human being who happened to be an absolute workaholic. I recognized this characteristic and quickly realized that I had to create boundaries, or this gig was not going to work. But, how and when to have the conversation was intimidating because I didn't want him to perceive me as disengaged or lazy. I risked jeopardizing my quality of personal life without clear lines between work and home.

Shortly after I started the job, in an attempt to be helpful, he said, "Melissa, I want you to know that I work 24 hours a day, seven days a week. If you need anything, and I mean anything at all, don't hesitate to pick up the phone and call me. I don't care if I'm on vacation or it's a weekend. If you need me, I'm here for you."

Boom! There it was my moment to set clear boundaries. I responded pleasantly yet deliberately, "Thank you so much for being so supportive and available, but I don't work 24 hours a day, seven days a week. My quality of life outside of work is even more important than my paycheck. So, can we agree to work together between 7:00 am and 5:00 pm Monday through Friday? Outside of those hours, I'm focused on my personal life." He understood and, I think, respected me even more for negotiating and being clear about my expectations.

I couldn't help but compare our working relationship with my peers. He had no boundaries as to when he would contact them – nights, weekends, PTO, etc. He expected that they would always be available. The lack of established boundaries festered into damaging misunderstandings about his disinterest in their well-being and personal lives. But that was an inaccurate assumption; he was extremely considerate but simply had a blind spot related to their needs. He worked around the clock, so he assumed they did, too, because they never said otherwise.

The relationship with my boss was one of the best I've ever experienced. Setting boundaries provided a sense of autonomy and trust, which improved my performance; it didn't diminish it.

Leaders, please understand how difficult it is for our team members to speak up and negotiate boundaries. Since it's so hard, we should eliminate the intimidation factor by initiating the boundary-setting discussion. The goal is to mutually establish expectations about how, when, and where you'll work together.

Are you proactively discussing boundaries with your team? Do you know what boundaries exist for them, or is it an unspoken expectation that whatever boundaries you expect are the ones they need to adhere to?

What's at stake if you don't proactively establish boundaries? Far too often, I've seen leaders lose their star players due to a lack of them. These star players typically surpass all performance expectations and prove they can handle anything we throw at them. So, what do we do? We assign more and more and more to the point that they burn out, and we lose our key contributors.

One of my coaching clients prides himself on being a high performer, loves his job, and respects his

Well Being

demanding boss, but he's become overwhelmed by the lack of balance in his life. His personal life is suffering, including the potential loss of his marriage due to work demands. He established core working hours but continues receiving emails from his boss during off hours, weekends, and vacations. He feels pressure to respond when these emails are received, inadvertently eroding his boundaries and causing further damage to his personal life.

If you were his coach, what advice would you give him?

Here's how it played out. He was committed to fixing his personal life but didn't want to quit his job. He deeply believed in the mission of the company but knew he'd have no choice if things didn't improve. So, he attempted a coaching-up conversation with his boss about the emails and expectations to respond. Although he was reluctant, he had nothing to lose at this point.

Help Them Thrive

Coaching up paid off. His boss was genuinely disappointed in herself for misreading their cues and unintentionally straining her team. She had no idea the emails were creating such an issue. Because the team members responded during off-hours, she assumed they were working too, so it was perfectly fine to contact them.

She responded with gratitude for his feedback and a solution that seemed reasonable in theory, but he knew it wasn't practical. "I work during off-hours and may send you emails, but please don't feel pressure to respond until you're back in the office. Problem solved!"

My client knew the boss's permission wasn't going to fix the problem. There is a sense of urgency that arises when a leader sends a note, so the team would still feel either pressure to respond or a chance to compete with their colleagues by attempting to prove they work harder than others.

He suggested a more practical solution that would solve the power-dynamic-influenced feeling of an obligation to respond even with the manager's permission not to. They'd all experienced managers who used that tactic as a test to sort out the "workers" from the "slackers."

My client responded to his boss with empathy and an assumption of good intent, "I trust you care deeply about our wellbeing and didn't intend for this to happen. May I suggest still sending the emails, but scheduling them to arrive during work hours? Doing so will eliminate any unintentional expectations of an immediate response. But let's be crisp in how we define this boundary. Exceptions will happen occasionally, so I recognize there will be times when we need to collaborate during off-hours." She liked that idea even better and thanked him for his courage, honesty, and feedback.

This simple tactic was incredibly effective and relieved my client from the immense pressure of feeling he needed to be accessible at all times. He is now thriving in life and at work.

Boundaries exist to help us thrive; negotiate them.

Not sure how to approach the boundary-setting conversation? Check out these helpful resources and then answer the questions below:

- Watch this video by TED Talks called Your 3-Step Guide to Set Better Boundaries and then use the prompts to define boundaries.

- Read the Forbes Article Have Trouble Setting Boundaries At Work? Try These 14 Expert Tips

What boundaries do you need to set for yourself so that you continue to thrive?

What boundaries have yet to be defined that would likely help your team thrive?

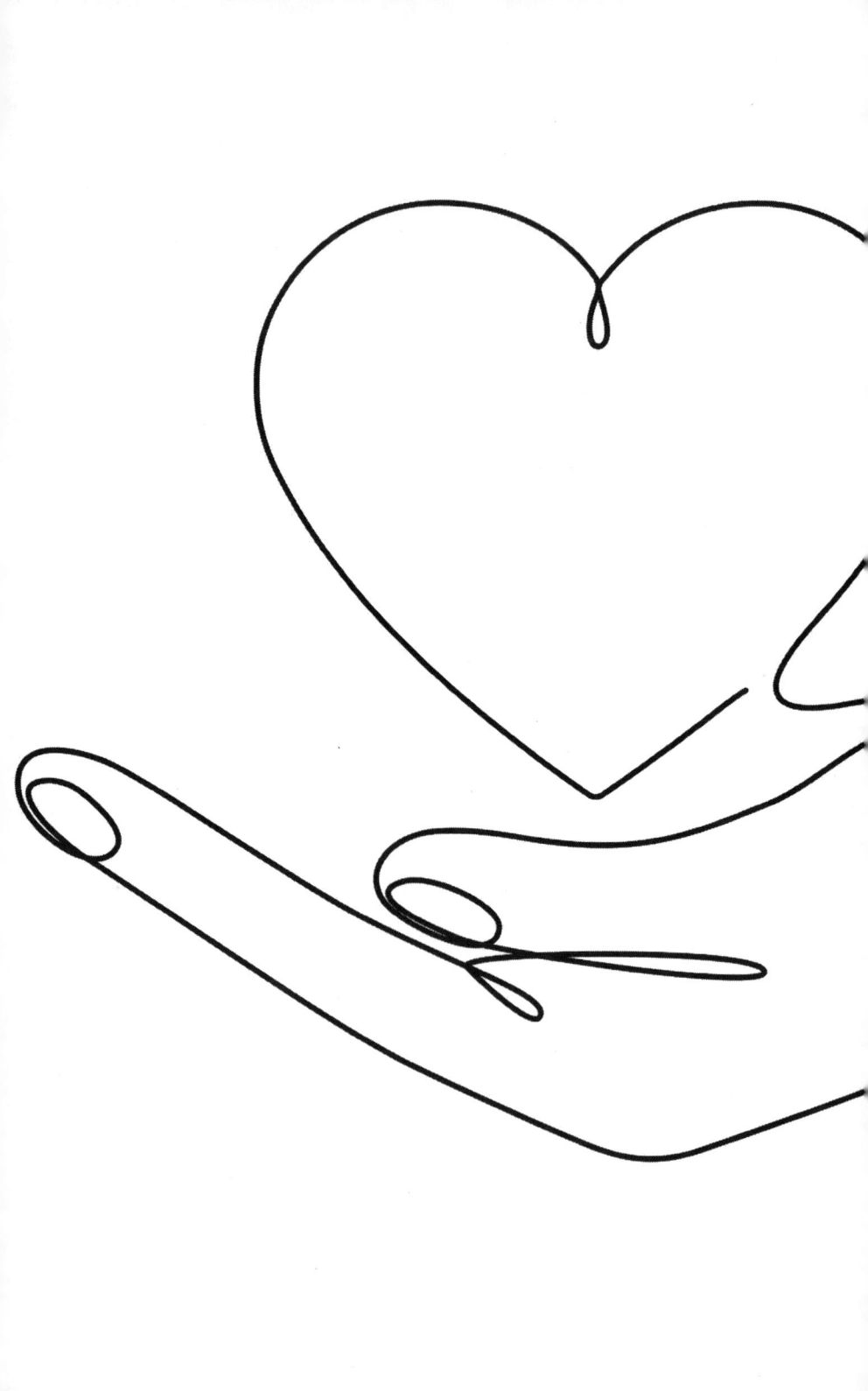

Chapter 4
PESKY EMOTIONS

During a recent keynote address, I threw my hand in the air and asked with anticipation and excitement, "Where are all the haters?" Of course, no one raised their hand; would you? I then proceeded to tell them this story in hopes it would change their minds and embrace being a ~~hater~~ human like me.

When I started my professional speaking career, I already had 20+ years of experience successfully speaking on large stages for the companies I'd worked for. The annual conference organizers for an association I was involved with were searching for speakers who were experts in

Help Them Thrive

leadership. "Sweet!" I was the perfect fit for what they needed. So, I threw my hat in the ring, which overjoyed the conference planning team, because they were confident that I would rock the house. But in the end, the head of the association felt like I "just wouldn't be good enough." Rejected. And I was feeling a way about it.

Nevertheless, I attended the conference. They selected another woman to be the keynote speaker, and I remember thinking she "just couldn't be *that* good." Sound familiar? Those pesky emotions; envy is especially sneaky.

I was feeling so funky about being rejected that I tried to avoid going to hear *her* ("*Her*" as in the unqualified speaker who took my spot). But it would be obvious if I wasn't in the room, so I reluctantly went to the session.

Friend, she *was* that good. I was in awe of everything about her - style, message, experience, and impact. As an emerging professional speaker, she modeled what excellence looked like on stage. My feelings of envy almost prevented me from going to hear her speak, and I would have missed out on lessons that continue to serve me now.

Because I experienced envy, does that make me a "hater"? No, it makes me human.

There are stigmas associated with emotions like envy, so we're reluctant to admit these feelings because the story we tell ourselves is we risk being permanently

Pesky Emotions

labeled. Others will assume these emotions are part of our character trait versus a temporary state of being.

I was gobsmacked while reading <u>The Atlas of the Heart</u> by Brené Brown. This book provides a much-needed vocabulary for feelings and emotional states that are difficult to identify and put into words. She explains how a person lacking this vocabulary lacks the ability to communicate their deepest desires, fears, and ambitions effectively.

All humans experience envy and jealousy from time to time, and typically, it arises when we see someone who has achieved what we want to achieve but we've yet to achieve it.

I've often witnessed envy show up at work, with lower-ranking, driven team members vying for the next level. Envy is often misdiagnosed as a personality flaw instead of the signal that a team member wants to achieve more but is likely misguided. What a terrific opportunity for us as leaders to redirect their energy in a positive manner. Provide stretch assignments and coaching to help them gain the experience they so greatly admire in others.

Do not, friend, I repeat, do not accuse others of being envious. That will only lead to defensiveness and fuel a potentially toxic dynamic. If you suspect jealousy or envy, ask,

Help Them Thrive

"I noticed you've taken a particular interest in x (person or role). Would you like to learn more about it and prepare to move into a similar position someday?"

Have you ever felt or suspected a colleague was feeling jealous or envious at work? If you could relive that experience, is there anything you would do differently to help yourself or the colleague shift their actions to result in a more positive outcome?

Discussing emotions at work can be taboo; as a result, many of us lack the practice to navigate them effectively. Helping humans thrive, including ourselves, requires us to acknowledge one of the fundamental aspects of being human – emotions.

So, how do emotions work? Essentially, our bodies have a physical reaction to an environmental condition – butterflies in the stomach, goosebumps, tensed muscles, etc. Then our bodies and brains try to make sense of the reaction.

"Hey, brain. What am I feeling right now?" Then, once the brain assesses the experience, it labels the emotion – happiness, anguish, fear, vulnerability, etc. It's a much more complex process, but no need to over-explain; I promised to keep it simple, friend.

So next month, I'm going to be on the biggest stage of my life. I will be speaking in front of thousands and thousands of people, the largest crowd I've ever been in front of, and I'm feeling a way about it. When I think about it, I feel a sensation in my belly and my heart rate increases. What emotion do you think I am feeling, *excitement* or *anxiety*?

The cool thing about these two emotions is excitement and anxiety show up in the same way within our bodies – increased blood pressure, butterflies in the tummy, and quickened heart rate. If our body's reaction is the same, and I label my feelings "anxiety." What do you think my preparation process will be like? I will likely avoid preparing because anxiety is negative and doesn't feel good. I'll likely procrastinate. It won't be something I look forward to, and I won't spend as much time prepping, so when it's showtime, I'll be under-prepared and nervous because I'm not confident in my performance.

In contrast, if I label the feeling "excitement," which feels good, I'll look forward to spending time preparing for

He was very fair-skinned, so it was visibly noticeable when he started to get defensive, even though he did his best to convey support and curiosity. Our warning sign was when his neck got red and splotchy. We would exchange glances, roll our eyes, and think, "He is so closed-minded. What a waste of time."

These brainstorming sessions typically resulted in a slight twist on the status quo versus new commitments to growth and innovation. His unchecked emotions had become the barrier to growth, not because he wasn't growth-minded, but because he blamed our "unoriginal, untenable ideas" as the root cause. In turn, we blamed him for being risk-averse and uncreative.

The truth is, he was ashamed of himself for not having the best ideas. His reaction was shame-driven, masked by defensive behavior. For many leaders, shame can be perceived as a sign of weakness, so we cope by projecting our shame onto others by blaming them.

As leaders, we often derive our value from feeling like we are the most experienced and most intelligent people in the room. And it doesn't help when many of our team members validate this by expecting us to have all the information and solutions to problems. An employee once said, "Melissa, you make the big bucks. Why are you asking my opinion? Don't you have all the answers?" This expectation may seem a bit ridiculous, but from my vantage point, it's more pervasive than we may be willing to admit.

As leaders, we want to feel like others can trust us to make the best decisions, often informed by knowledge and insight others don't have. If we don't have the most brilliant ideas, it can call our value into question.

One of my coaching clients is the CEO of a mid-sized, global investment firm based in California. In a discussion about the correlation between perceived leader value and shame, he talked about the pressure of being a leader and living up to the expectations that are cast upon him.

He said, "Honestly, Melissa, the biggest risk is our insecurity. Even though many of us won't admit this, when lower-ranked people have different opinions and are proved right where we were wrong, it feels like my value is in question. Earning and keeping trust requires that employees believe in our logic and decisions. So, when they have better ideas than me, it feels like a threat to my position and success as a leader."

He reluctantly admitted that it's more comfortable to be surrounded by "Yes-People" who make us feel like hyper-intelligent leaders compared to those who challenge our ideas.

Being surrounded by people who always agree seduces many into an unhealthy "All-Knowing" mindset. This

5. Prioritize curiosity over being right.

These steps will lead to psychologically safe environments where humans don't feel they need to dumb themselves down to preserve a relationship with their leader. Consistently demonstrating these steps will lead to team members who don't fear backlash when sharing innovative ideas and potential risks. There's too much at stake to allow unchecked shame to get in the way of growth.

Let's reflect on how well we demonstrate the 5 Steps. Next to each step, rate how well you demonstrate these actions.

Actions	Rating (1 = No, 10 = Yes)
I admit to others that I don't have all the answers.	
I establish and reiterate the expectation that others' voices and ideas matter, and I expect them to speak up..	
I encourage contrarian opinions.	
I know my physiological warning signs that indicate I'm getting defensive.	
I prioritize curiosity over being right.	

What unique insights has this activity sparked for you?

Pesky Emotions

There was a time in my career when I was thriving yet left a job I loved. It fell apart primarily due to the havoc wreaked by a leader's unintentional, unacknowledged feelings of envy and threat.

Let's rewind to when I started the job 2.5 years before I chose the nuclear option of resigning. This job was an absolute turnaround gig. Talk about your fixer-upper! Everything needed to be reinvented and optimized – products, services, processes, people, etc.

When I came on board, the company was prepared to shut down the entire division if we didn't quickly turn our results around in revenue, profitability, product quality, and service levels. Everything and everyone needed to be improved.

When I interviewed for the job, the hiring manager said, "I really like you and will likely extend an offer to you. But let me be crisp: if you don't turn this team around in a year, you won't be here, and no one on your team will either. Are you still interested in the job?" I confidently responded, "A complex challenge is precisely what I am looking for. And don't worry, I'll still be here with the rest of my team in a year."

And we did exactly what I promised we'd do; we surpassed all our goals and reinvigorated the team. The great news was we were getting attention and accolades for our success; the bad news was we were getting attention and accolades for our success.

What I had done with my team landed on the radar of a very senior executive within the firm. Out of curiosity, they went to my boss, their peer, and asked if they could meet with me and hear all about our best practices.

So, he came to me and asked if I would mind meeting with this leader. Which I was happy to do. I admired what her team had done, which was tangential to our work. It didn't overlap, but there were similarities in the type of outcomes we were expected to achieve.

Within minutes, I could sense that she felt threatened by my team's success. You see, I was a lower-ranking employee, but I was out-pacing her team in terms of performance, which she perceived as a threat. Emotionally, what was happening was she was envious but didn't catch it and thus allowed envy to control her actions.

After the call, I asked my boss if his peer had given him any indication that she wanted to assume responsibility for my team; he responded, "Oh no, we have a great relationship. She wouldn't dare make a move like that without proactively talking to me. She has her hands full with her existing division. I can't imagine that she wants anything to do with yours, but I'll keep my eyes open for it just in case."

In just a few short weeks following that conversation, he gets a call from an even more prominent executive, who tells him that going forward, my team would report to his peer; you know, the one he trusted and never suspected would make such a move. Yeah, that one.

He came to me disgusted, angry, and embarrassed that he didn't see it coming. He regretted trusting her and would have worked harder to retain ownership of my team but was out-maneuvered by an envy-fueled leader.

Within the first week of reporting to my new boss, she came to me and said, "Melissa, you're the key to the future of this division; what you have created here is a model for us all. What I want you to do now is find a way to outsource your entire division to one of the offshore partners you have brought on to help you expand and scale. You're vital to defining the path for this outsourcing initiative."

My question back to her was, "What problem are we trying to solve here? Our margin is exceptional, and our products and services are better than ever." She couldn't answer the question intelligently because there wasn't a business problem to solve. The real issue was related to envy and a leader who felt threatened by a lower-ranking employee's success.

At that time, I didn't see it that way. What I perceived was an inept, uninformed leader who lacked vision and made poor decisions. So, I went home and pondered the situation over the weekend, came back on Monday, and I told her that, although in theory, her idea seemed wise, it was untenable.

My division was a microcosm of the entire company. Part of it could be outsourced, which I'd already done, but the whole division could not. Then I told her that, in addition to the impracticality of that decision, I was not—the type of leader who would turn around and sabotage the careers of this team. A team who'd worked their asses off followed my vision on blind faith and progressed from a failing squad to one that had achieved double-digit growth and was surpassing 35% profitability.

She was going to have to find someone else to do that job - I was not that kind of leader.

Within 90 short days, the team imploded. The entire function was scattered and decentralized across the organization. The service, revenue, profitability, and morale all eroded. The division failed, not due to a lack of performance but because a well-intentioned leader allowed envy to influence her thoughts and behavior, which led to adverse reputational, financial, and service impacts for the organization.

Envy doesn't just happen to lower-ranking workers eager to climb the ladder. Envy often seduces unsuspecting, well-established leaders into feeling that their value is threatened when others thrive, thus coping by mitigating the perceived threat to feel more secure.

You might be tempted to vilify this leader and label her a power-hungry, blankety-blank who got away with wrecking an entire division. No, wait, those were my thoughts at the time. Ha!! I'm human, y'all; of course, I was upset.

I was sad and concerned for my former team. I grieved the joy that came with achieving goals no one thought possible. I missed my colleagues. I was still in love with the mission and promise of the company.

Feeling angry came naturally, but I refused to stay in that state for long. The longer you stay tangled in feelings like this, the harder it is to get untangled. So, how did I pull myself out? With a purposeful pivot. It's when you decide to intentionally learn from tragedy and glean wisdom from your or others' failures. The phrase I use to purposefully pivot is this,

"What is the leadership lesson I should learn from this situation?"

Forcing yourself to answer this question will lead to insights that enable you to cultivate wisdom from failure. We can't change the past, but we can certainly learn from it.

Help Them Thrive

In this situation, I learned how easy it was to judge other leaders and accuse them of having inherently bad characters when mistakes happen. As humans, we're wired to be judgmental, so it can be amusing and honestly energizing to tear down those who have caused us harm. But at what cost? Doing so made me feel powerless and victimized. Purposefully pivoting allowed me to recognize that I could find myself in the same position of having my logic and rationale hijacked by emotions. We've all been there and will be there again.

So how do we regain our logic and rational thinking when we feel threatened?

Let's refresh our earlier discussion on what happens when the brain is in a state of threat, like what happened to the leader we're discussing. The amygdala's intense emotional response often overrides the prefrontal cortex, leading us to act impulsively rather than rationally.

There are leadership lessons to be learned from this experience. One of the most important is to learn how to properly manage and mitigate our emotions from controlling our behavior.

This simple four-step process serves as a hack to help you navigate your emotions and mitigate behavior that you'll regret when your brain is back to normal.

Pesky Emotions

Step One: **Recognize that your body is having a reaction to a situation.**

"I'm having a reaction to something that is happening. My neck is itchy, and my jaw is clenched."

Step Two: **Correctly label your emotions.**

Think, "I'm feeling an emotion. Precisely, what is it?"

If the emotion is one that may transition your brain into a state of threat, take a deep breath through your nose. Next, inhale a bit more air. It may feel like your lungs are already full but try to expand them even more. Hold it in for a moment, and then slowly exhale through your mouth. Filling your lungs with air sends a signal to your brain that you're safe and will help put your brain back into a normal state, so you can regain control of your logic and rational thinking.

Step Three: Choose supportive actions.

Ask yourself, "How can I help them thrive?"

That is how you pivot negative emotions into something that has a positive outcome for others. Intentionally choose actions that will help others thrive.

Step Four: Reflect and improve.

Regularly reflect on your behavior and notice the contrast between your actions and thoughts when you were in a normal state of mind vs. a threat state.

Try to really hear the stories you tell yourself about others in both states of mind. Often when we feel threatened, we'll convince ourselves that our retaliatory actions are justified to cope with feelings of guilt or regret.

Ask, "I demonstrated my interest in their success." Or "I may have acted irrationally. What will I do the next time I'm in this situation?"

Remember my story about feeling envious of that accomplished speaker? Friend, since that experience, I have referred more business to her than I can count. Negative feelings don't have to result in negative actions.

You can leverage them as triggers to make conscious choices that help others thrive.

Think about a time when you were likely in a "threat state" and acted irrationally. Based on what we've discussed, if you could relive that moment, what would you do differently?

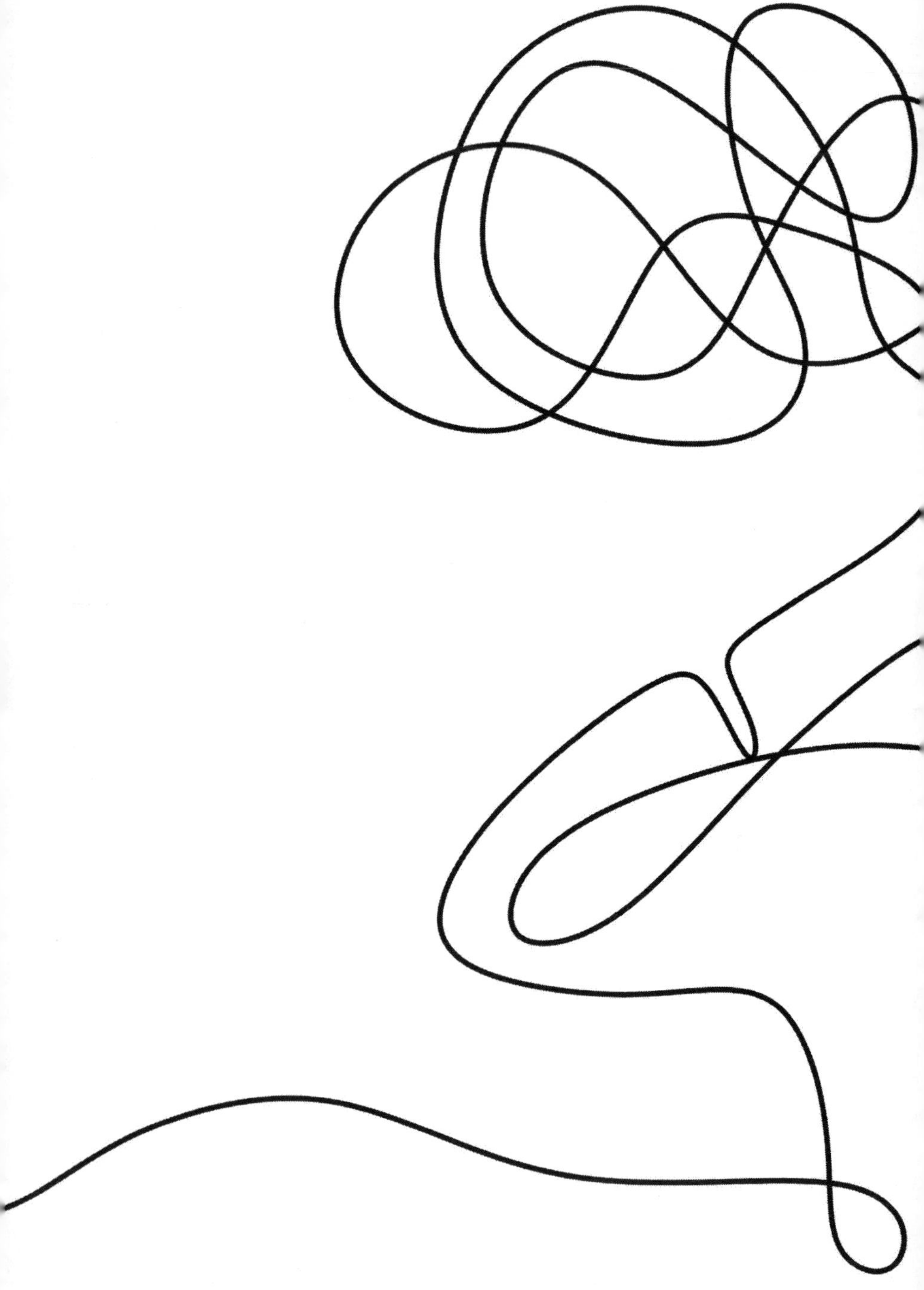

Chapter 5
CONFUSING FEEDBACK

I'll open this discussion with a question, are you a great feedback *giver*?

1	2	3	4	5	6	7	8	9	10

1 = Not really.   10 = Yes.

Are you a great feedback *receiver*?

1	2	3	4	5	6	7	8	9	10

1 = Not really.   10 = Yes.

One of my many childhood memories includes my mom saying, "If you can't say anything nice, don't say anything at all!" Ha! Did you hear this phrase too? So often, when I'm about to give feedback, especially constructive feedback, that unnerving phrase will pop into my mind.

Many leaders are reluctant to give feedback for a myriad — potential receiver defensiveness, damaged relationships, a fear it won't be received well, or, the most common barrier, it's uncomfortable, and we suck at it, so we avoid it.

Feedback is like a flashlight in the dark. It reduces the risk of tripping over things we can't see.

If we as leaders don't shine a light on those barriers and obstacles, our teammates and colleagues will continue to trip over things they cannot see. This ultimately leads to lackluster performance simply because we didn't illuminate their path.

Have you ever canceled an employee? What I mean by "canceling" is to avoid the uncomfortable and complicated process of coaching and feedback; instead, mentally add the employee to a layoff waitlist, tolerate their poor performance until the time comes, and then terminate them. Easy, right? No personal guilt for firing (instead, we blame financial performance or whatever reasoning is being peddled for the mass layoff), no tedious performance management plans…no compassion, no feedback, and no leadership.

I'm noticing more well-intentioned, kind leaders opting into canceling instead of coaching employees. Although a seemingly convenient way to cut through HR red tape, this practice creates long-term toxicity in the workplace.

One of my coaching clients recently said, "I have given feedback to this employee on a few occasions, and his behavior hasn't changed. I've tried to coach him, but I've given up. He is a problem and needs to leave."

My response to him was, "Are you certain he comprehended your feedback and precisely understood what you expected? Perhaps confusion, not inability, is to blame for the lack of behavior change."

Let's be honest; most of us struggle with providing actionable and comprehensible feedback. We're often unintentionally ambiguous and spark defensiveness in the receiver, which causes their brain to shift into a threat state rather than being open-minded. When someone gets defensive, their brain deregulates and can't think clearly. Conversely, if we're uncomfortable or nervous when giving feedback, our messages are likely confusing. No wonder performance doesn't improve after a feedback session!

There's hope, friend. Giving feedback doesn't have to be uncomfortable and discouraging. But often, these conversations go sideways and don't result in behavior change. It's no wonder many of us have fallen into the cycle of canceling employees; it can seem like the easier choice. Perhaps on the front end, yet it spills long-lasting toxicity into the environment for those remaining.

"Employees who stay at a company after layoffs often feel anxiety around the future of the company," said Kathryn Minshew, founder, and CEO of The Muse, a career development platform. "It can be hard because most employers can't or won't comment on why certain people were chosen for layoffs and others weren't."

Of course, they can't comment because often, the logic is subjective based on the decision-maker's thoughts about the workers' performance. Suppose the selection of the laid-off employee makes sense to others and is anticipated based on measurable data like missed goals or damaging behavior. In that case, less damage is done to the psyche of the survivors. They typically accept the decision.

However, when seemingly good performers get laid off, leaving the remaining surprised and confused, it evokes thoughts like,

"I'm next, so why should I work so hard?"

"They aren't loyal to us; why should I be loyal to them?"

"The heart has left this place. Leadership doesn't care about us anymore."

"I can't work in this toxic environment. I'm resigning now so I can leave on my terms."

"I don't trust them with my future."

Continuous layoff cycles are like oil spills. They leak pollutants into our work environment. We've all seen those heart-breaking images of animals covered in oil struggling to survive after an unintentional oil spill. Similarly, layoff survivors get coated in performance-inhibiting toxins that make it difficult to thrive – anxiety, loss of trust, and post-traumatic stress. These toxins, unlike oil, are undetectable to the eye. The evidence shows up in degraded customer experiences, disengagement, and turnover.

I am not suggesting you retain poor performers to avoid the consequences of survivor guilt. I've always believed that you have two options in managing subpar performers – coach up or coach out. Retaining poor performers to avoid dealing with cumbersome firing processes or the discomfort of coaching creates toxins too.

We may not have control over mass layoffs, but we can ensure everyone on our team is receiving actionable coaching that illuminates success barriers and hedges against the temptation to "cancel" them.

I've curated a simple yet profoundly impactful framework on how to give feedback in a brain-friendly way that yields better performance and behavior change. This brilliant yet simple approach comes from the genius mind and research of Cognitive Psychologist LeeAnn Renniger.

She has designed a four-part formula for giving feedback well: starting with a "micro-yes" question to signal feedback, providing specific data points, stating the impact of those points, and concluding with a question for engagement.

Please scan this QR code to watch the video before reading the next segment.

One of my favorite aspects of leading and coaching is helping others maximize their potential. Nothing thrills me more than to witness people achieve their dreams and experience the joy and fulfillment that come with embracing our talents.

Friend, as leaders, we typically don't receive feedback on how we can become better, so how *can* we become better? I won't belabor the difficulties of coaching but will underscore that coaching up is even harder to do. As a result, we often lack the insight needed to maximize our leadership impact.

Oftentimes, we receive information on our performance after a team member has resigned. This feedback can come from the exit interview or the rumor mill; either way, it's too late to course correct. We, as leaders, are so in the dark because people tell us what they think we want to hear versus what needs to be said, thanks to the power dynamics at play.

Typically, leaders have the power to either make or break employee's careers, so often, team members choose the less risky route by stroking their egos or saying nothing. How can we improve without feedback?

LeeAnn Renniger talks about "pull feedback," where we regularly ask for thoughts on our performance. Asking for feedback provides space and permission for our teams to coach up. But how is it done?

I want to offer a "pull feedback" hack for you. Pose this question to your colleagues,

"What can I do to support you even better?"

Let's break down the logic behind this question. It establishes that you aren't currently doing anything wrong; you simply want to innovate and improve, and you desire their insight.

When receiving the response to this question, be sure to recognize your defensive and emotional triggers. Pay attention to your body language when you have this exchange with your colleagues. Be physically positioned in a manner that conveys safety and a genuine interest in their thoughts. Be very, very careful not to get defensive. Deeply listen to understand, not defend.

Help Them Thrive

> Vanessa Van Edwards is one of my favorite body language experts. Her article on aggressive body language is useful and makes me giggle. Check it out for some great tips!

After receiving the feedback, acknowledge how difficult it probably was for them to share. Tell them that you're grateful and that you trust their feedback is coming from a place of caring and not judgment.

If you ask enough colleagues for feedback, you will likely start to identify trends and themes that you can prioritize and act upon. For example, if multiple people say you're a perpetual interrupter, then, friend, you are probably a perpetual interrupter. I can speak to this particular example because that is precisely the feedback trend that I uncovered from my team a few years ago. It stung when I received it, but it was still a gift nonetheless. Now that I'm aware, I am much more cognizant of interrupting others.

Think of a colleague who needs feedback on their behavior. Using LeeAnn Renniger's Four-Part, Brain-Friendly Feedback Formula, script what you should say to this colleague.

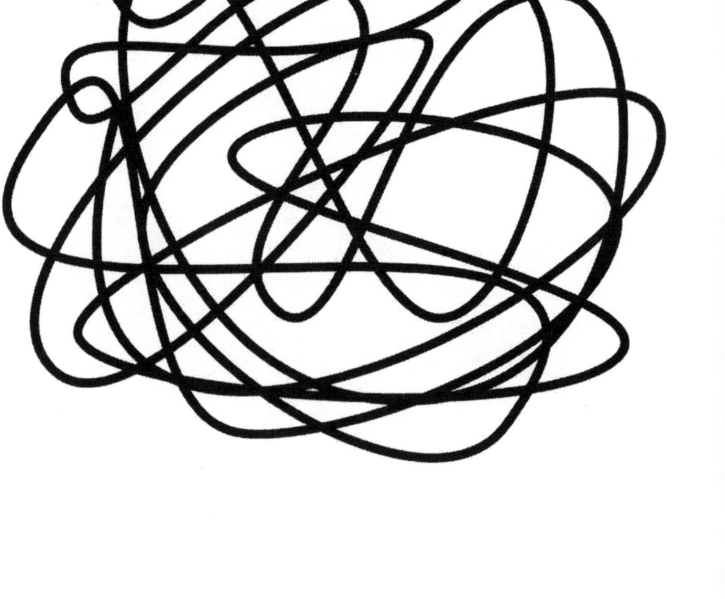

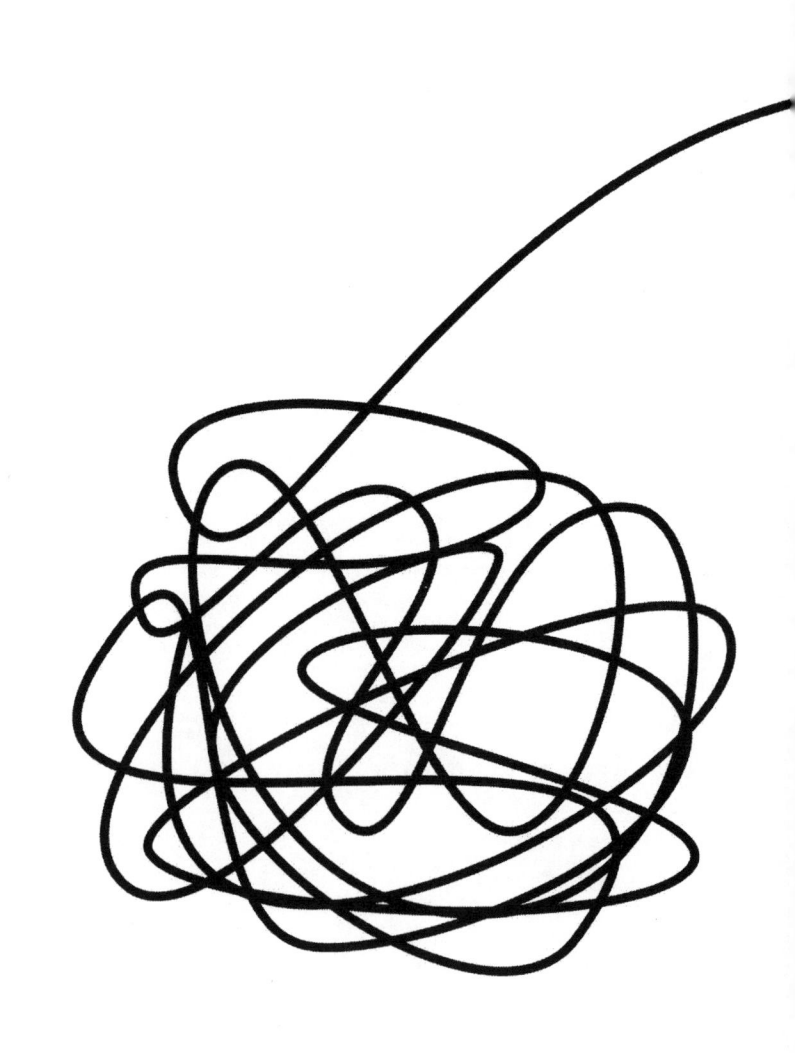

Chapter 6
DECLUTTER THE WORKLOAD

"We support how many products?"

"85 products."

"And we design, maintain, and provide service on all 85?"

"Yes, that's correct."

"Wow, that's a lot of work for such a small team! Small, but mighty, huh?"

"That's what they call us. But, in reality, we're spread too thin."

"Which products do clients use the most?"

"Most clients regularly use these 10 products. The remainder get less than 15 users per year."

"So, why do we maintain 75 products with such low usage rates?"

"Because we've always done it that way."

I just love hearing that phrase, "Because we've always done it that way." Why do I love it so much? Because it instantly illuminates a team's clutter. It also makes me think about hoarding. Here's the Mayo Clinic's definition of hoarding.

> *Hoarding disorder is an ongoing difficulty in throwing away or parting with possessions because you believe that you need to save them. You may experience distress at the thought of getting rid of the items. You gradually keep or gather a huge number of items, regardless of their actual value.*

Lots of us have become hoarders at work and don't realize it. Many of our teams are burning out, not because of toxic behavior but rather due to the continuous cycle of doing more with less. Which in theory, means to become more efficient. In practice, it means doing more work with fewer people.

Our teams shrink, and then we simply scatter the remnants of former employees' workloads across the remaining

Declutter The Workload

team. Rinse and repeat. A tipping point exists where a team will buckle and break down due to the unbearable load of work and tasks. This dynamic is, essentially, the proverbial straw that breaks the camel's back. Do you proactively know which straw will break them down? Nope. We typically find out when it's too late.

Think of a hoarder's closet stuffed full of clothes they have collected over the years. In time, the bar that holds the hanging clothes begins to bend, then crack, and eventually break due to the overwhelming load.

How do we remedy this situation? We need to tidy the junk out of our workloads. Let's be honest; like shopping, it's much more fun to get new stuff. Our beloved brainstorming sessions are like shopping sprees at work.

We gather around a conference table with sweet goodies that the boss sprung for to get our creative juices flowing with a sugar rush. The leader then shares some inspiring speech on how we need to think outside the box and assures us there are no wrong answers. We gladly start spewing all sorts of cool and innovative products and services we could offer. Yay, how much fun is this! We happily commit to new work, thus stuffing another item into our already overflowing closet.

Rarely during these sessions do we discuss removing items to make room for the new ones. Shopping is much more fun than organizing, so why spend time on that?

Help Them Thrive

We accumulate more and more stuff, just like that pair of skinny jeans that haven't been worn in 10 years but still has a spot in the closet.

When was the last time you participated in a "purging" meeting to identify work clutter that bogs us down and adds little value? Given the increasing rates of workers feeling stressed and overwhelmed, purging discussions should happen more frequently than brainstorming ones if we want to create bandwidth for our teams to focus on the stuff that truly matters.

One of my favorite organizing experts is Marie Kondo; she's like the tidy goddess of Netflix. If you're unfamiliar with her, I highly recommend that you check out some of her shows. Essentially, she comes into people's homes and guides them on how to purge, create space, and experience the peace that comes with letting go. If items don't spark joy for the owners, they thank them for serving them and then remove the item. People have a myriad of reasons why they hold on to their stuff, whether it's sentimental or just hope they may use it again in the future. She logically guides them through analyzing the true value of their belongings. This rational approach typically releases them from the emotional and irrational attachments they have to certain items, so they can purge without regret.

Declutter The Workload

You cannot be strategic without space in your day to pause, ponder, and plan. You cannot have clarity of thought, speeding between tasks, meetings, and emails all day long. And the only way you can add time into your day is by eliminating things that don't continue to serve you, your company, or your team.

Good thing there's a hack for that! Regularly ask your team this question, **"What should we start, stop, or continue doing?"**

The responses will reveal trends and priorities for growth, pain points, and purging. We must intentionally create space to increase bandwidth and reduce the likelihood of our teams feeling overwhelmed.

A friend of mine (let's call him Carl) recently resigned from his job managing logistics, fulfillment, and maintenance for a leading coffee roasting company. He was fed up with being overwhelmed with "busy work" that added no real value.

In his first few years on the job, he was an absolute superstar performer. He was in love with the mission of the company, enjoyed the challenges of a growing firm, and was willing to do whatever was needed to support the success of the company. I don't think I've ever met someone so proud of the work they did. His enthusiasm for the company was infectious, and he spread pride to his colleagues and the customers he served.

Help Them Thrive

During the pandemic, the company had to furlough most of its employees. Carl was still working but was only allowed to work half-time. That didn't matter to Carl. He had so much pride in the company and cared about the clients that he continued to work full-time even though he wasn't getting paid. (Close your ears, my HR friends.)

He continued to handle all the tasks that his former team had been doing. He was often the only one in the office, except for the CEO, who was also there trying to keep operations afloat despite the extreme challenges. Neither one of them minded, as they were both former military and viewed the pandemic as a time of war; you do whatever is needed to win.

Like most businesses after the pandemic, revenue returned, purchasing volume increased, customers became more active, etc. Now that "wartime" had ended, Carl needed help. He couldn't continue at the same pace without resources. His portfolio of responsibilities had become bogged down with so many tasks that there wasn't enough time or bandwidth for him to complete projects that would result in higher value for the firm.

He asked for resources and was repeatedly denied. Through his willingness to go above and beyond, this "superstar" inadvertently conditioned them to believe he would never become overwhelmed. He already proved he could do more with less, so they continued to add

Declutter The Workload

more and more. He couldn't help to compare how his pleas for resources were denied while others, seemingly less vital, were approved.

He had zero bandwidth for more work and felt unappreciated and used. The pride he once had for his company evaporated, and he became angry and cynical. In time, he resigned from his job, and now the company pays four times his salary to a managed services firm for the same work.

There's an apex to cycles of efficiency. Continuously doing more with less can lead to workload clutter and overwhelm employees who cannot thrive under the weight of an unbearable load. Purge, friend. Purge.

Think about your own workload. List three tasks or projects that may not add the value they should, but you continue to do them anyway.

_____
_____
_____
_____
_____
_____
_____
_____

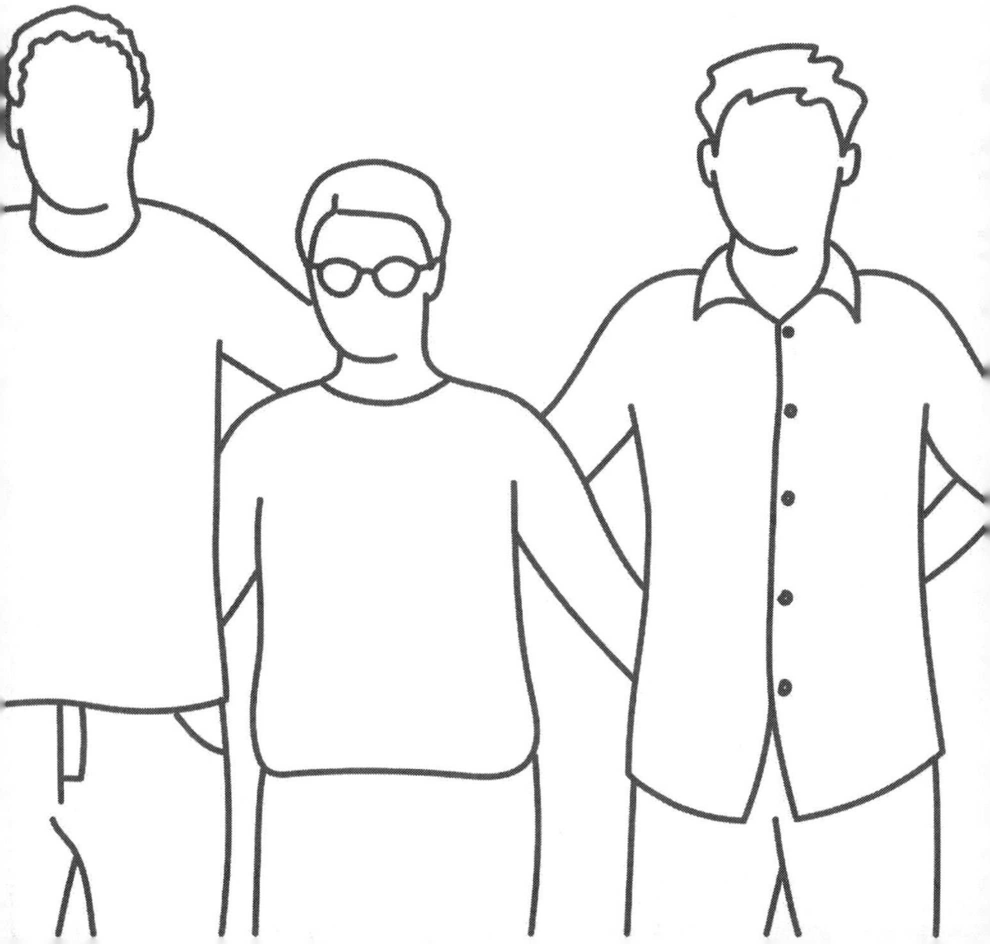

Chapter 7
HUMANS NEED FRIENDS

What if I told you? I helped two leaders who hated each other become friends in less than 45 minutes. Would you believe me? Well, you should. I know it seems unlikely, but it happened. All thanks to a scientifically proven, brilliant, yet simple method for helping people connect on a human level beyond their differences.

Before we proceed, name two colleagues who have a contentious relationship that, if improved, would reduce toxic dynamics at work. Who are they?

Person 1:

Person 2:

OK, keep them in mind as you read about this next story. I was recently doing deep leadership and cultural optimization work with the senior leadership team of a US-based firm with around 3,000 employees. Part of my services included one-on-one and group coaching with the executives.

It was widely known that the head of product development and the head of sales had a strained relationship. Although they were amicable during meetings, tension was palpable and their interactions were dysfunctional and uncomfortable. This negativity trickled down to their respective teams, leading to poor collaboration and dysfunction throughout the company.

They always disagreed and constantly interrupted each other. They never sat in close proximity, and the negative feelings these two leaders had toward each other leaked onto their teams. Hence, the dysfunction and poor collaboration cascaded down throughout the ranks.

So, not only did these leaders clash due to loyalty to their leader, but it normalized their team's clashing as well. This dynamic festered into an "us versus them" siloed experience between their teams.

One of the expectations the CEO had for my work with them was to improve trust amongst the senior leadership team. All the other members had a reasonably healthy relationship except for these two. Their contentious relationship often distracted this executive team from focusing on what mattered because they were tangled up in unproductive outcomes and conflicts that led to lackluster decisions, rework, and miscommunication.

During my privileged time serving as their coach, the individual leaders, in one-on-one coaching sessions, felt safe to share their unvarnished opinions on this relationship. They revealed to me how contentious their toxic relationship had become and that it needed to be resolved.

You see, in the safety of confidential coaching conversations, these leaders were willing to share their concerns and true feelings about one another. They also discussed and revealed aspects of their respective personal life challenges. Oddly enough, I discovered that they were much more alike than different. But how could I get them to realize their commonalities without sacrificing confidentiality?

The only way to repair their relationship would require vulnerability and personal disclosure, which seemed unlikely. If they could bond on a human level beyond the established and expected tension that was between them, they might become friends and even better peers.

This would drastically improve dynamics in terms of collaboration between their two teams, better products, more realistic revenue goals, go-to-market plans, timelines, etc.

So, during an offsite leadership retreat, I paired the leaders up with one another and strategically assigned the two "oil and water" colleagues to each other. I then presented them with an exercise that is based on Psychologist Arthur Aron's work on expanded relationships.

Arthur Aron, PhD, is a research professor of psychology at Stony Brook University. He is an APA fellow and has spent decades studying how people develop and maintain close relationships, particularly romantic relationships. He developed the self-expansion model of relationships, which posits that one main motivation for forming relationships with others is our own personal growth: Relationships allow us to grow and expand our sense of self. Outside of academia, Aron is perhaps best known for developing "The 36 Questions that Lead to Love."

I tweaked Aron's 36 Questions that Lead to Love and customized them for professional relationships. One of the leaders who participated called this a "vulnerability hack" that rapidly deepens relationships in a non-threatening way.

During this exercise, you gradually reveal close, sustained, escalating, reciprocal, personal self-disclosure. Most of us don't have experience doing that, especially at work. So, we need help, and this is just the guide we need.

Conduct the exercise with another person or a small group. Interview each other using the questions as a guide. Note that both people should answer each question before proceeding to the next. I recommend setting aside at least one hour to complete the exercise.

Want a printable version of these questions? I'm happy to share. Scan this QR code to access it on the Help Them Thrive Resources page.

Here are the questions:

Set I

1. Given the choice of anyone worldwide, whom would you want as a dinner guest?
2. Before making a telephone call, do you ever rehearse what you will say? Why?
3. What would constitute a "perfect" day for you?
4. When did you last sing to yourself? To someone else?

5. If you could live to the age of 90 and retain either the mind or body of a 30-year-old for the last 60 years of your life, which would you want?

6. Do you have a secret hunch about how you will die?

7. For what in your life do you feel most grateful?

8. If you could change anything about how you were raised, what would it be?

9. Take four minutes and tell your partner your life story in as much detail as possible.

10. If you could wake up tomorrow having gained any one quality or ability, what would it be?

Set II

11. What would you want to know if a crystal ball could tell you the truth about yourself, your life, the future, or anything else?

12. Is there something that you've dreamed of doing for a long time? Why haven't you done it?

13. What is the greatest accomplishment of your life?

14. What is your most treasured memory?

15. If you knew that in one year you would die suddenly, would you change anything about the way you are now living? Why?

16. Do you feel your childhood was happier than most others?
17. Describe a time when you witnessed someone being mistreated a work, and you didn't handle it well. What would you do differently if you could relive that experience?

Set III

18. If you were to become a close friend with your partner, please share what would be vital for them to know.
19. Share with your partner an embarrassing moment in your life.
20. What, if anything, is too severe to be joked about?
21. Share a personal problem and ask your partner for advice. Also, ask your partner to reflect on how you feel about your chosen situation.

Once the interview is complete, take 15 minutes by yourself to think. You can go for a walk or find a quiet place alone to reflect on your conversation. Ponder insights, newly discovered commonalities, and how this information changes your thinking about your colleague.

So, the leaders I mentioned spent an hour conducting this interview with one another. After the interviews, we all returned to the board room to debrief and share the unique insight they gained during the exercise.

The most amazing thing happened! One of the two "oil and water" leaders said, "I learned more about my colleague in the last 45 minutes than I had in the previous four years, and because of this experience, we discovered that we are both facing similar challenges in our personal lives. We acknowledged that we needed each other's counsel. I feel relieved and optimistic."

Yes! You see, they finally connected beyond their differences. I love it when a plan comes together.

These results seem magical, but the process is not magic; it's backed by the science of Arthur Aron's work on the self-expansion model of relationships. How can our relationships deepen if our typical conversations don't facilitate empathy for others? No wonder we suffer with so many tense work relationships that rarely improve; they just worsen and create a ripple effect with others. Relationships don't heal or expand without meaningful dialogue.

Usually, our work conversations are so transactional that connecting on a human level beyond superficial insights is rare.

"Did you get my email?"

"Did you send the invoice?"

"Where is the meeting going to be held?

Evolving beyond transactional to meaningful conversations takes intentionality, mindfulness, and questions that facilitate self-disclosure. Revealing shared interests, values, and experiences enables us to be more understanding, empathetic, curious, and honest. The closer we feel to others, the more likely we are to view them as friends versus foes. I discuss the "us vs them" mentality extensively in my book, The Seven Simple Habits of Inclusive Leaders. There, I explain how we can unintentionally treat people we perceive as an "us" with curiosity rather than judgment. With the "thems," we can unwittingly criticize versus empathize.

As leaders, unhealthy relationships with our peers become contagious and can infect our entire organization. Our direct reports often feel loyal to their leader and compelled to take sides. As humans, we are biologically wired for social connection and belonging. We need to feel understood and belong to social groups as much as we need to eat. It's that important to our survival and ability to thrive.

Silos commonly exist, and we as leaders can define the lines between "us versus them," unintentionally labeling, through our actions, behavior, and language, who our teams should deem as the adversary. Once the enemy character is established, in our psyches, we find it easier

Help Them Thrive

to justify their mistreatment, especially during extreme times of stress or threat; think of wars.

Consider the conflicts happening around the world. Which side of these conflicts do you empathize with more? You likely empathize more with the people you perceive as "us" versus the opposite side - the adversaries, the "thems." Consider the inhumane treatment that takes place on both sides of the conflict. When the "thems" experience this treatment, does it bother you as much?

I recently watched the latest Top Gun movie with my family. Spoiler alert: I'm going to reveal some details that took place. Don't worry, though. If you haven't watched it yet, I won't ruin the experience for you.

During the film, there is a scene that clearly defines the antagonists from the protagonists. The "good guys" are the characters we follow throughout the entire movie. We know their stories, empathize with their experience, and hope they will prevail. The "bad guys" we know nothing about, other than one of our trusted "good guys" said they are the enemy. We're entirely oblivious to their mission, lives, or culture.

The opposing teams get into a "dog flight" after the "good guys" bomb their base. During the fight, we witnessed one of the "good guys'" jets get hit by a missile, and I remember feeling a sense of remorse as sorrowful music played in the background. All production aspects were designed to evoke the same feelings within us all – remorse for the good guys and hatred for the bad.

In contrast, during the same scene, one of the bad guys' jets is blown to smithereens. Everyone at the watch party yelled, "Yay!!" We were all awash with an extreme sense of patriotism and hope.

There's another side to that story, though, isn't there? It didn't take much to coax us into hating the enemy. All we needed to know was that one of the good guys said we should hate them, so we did. We perceive the good guy as an "us" and, as a result, instantly view a "them," someone we know nothing about, as the enemy.

Threading this concept back to leadership, if we tell our teams that someone else is a "them," they usually align their viewpoints with ours whether they genuinely agree or simply want to maintain a good relationship with us. When this occurs, workers start behaving as if the other person or team is untrustworthy, which wrecks collaboration and toxifies the work environment.

I don't know about you, but I'm a huge fan of Ted Lasso. If you're not yet a Ted Lasso fan, let me give you a quick overview of this clever series on Apple TV. The show is about an American-based football coach who essentially gets duped into accepting a position to serve as a manager of the FC Richmond soccer team in England. The franchise owner wants to sabotage the team just to spite her ex-husband, so she chooses unsuspecting Ted. Unbeknownst to him, she felt he would be the perfect ringer to ruin the FC Richmond team and deliver the ultimate revenge on her ex-husband.

When Ted Lasso first arrived in Richmond, he stood out in every possible way, from his distinctly American accent with a Southern drawl to his dislike for England's favorite drink, tea, to his ever-positive outlook even in the face of failure.

As you can imagine, the fans, the team, and everyone in Richmond treats him like an outcast. They are beyond cruel to him. Yet and still, he perseveres and continues unapologetically revealing his humanity. Their mistreatment of him doesn't dim his light. He has an unshakable hope in humanity, and through consistent positivity and grace, he ultimately turns this community of "us versus them" into a community of "we."

Check out one of my favorite clips from Ted Lasso. Scan this QR code to watch it.

In the clip, he hustles a bully in a game of darts. During the dart match, he quotes Walt Wittman and says, "Be curious, not judgmental." He describes how the people who've viewed him as an "other" underestimated him his entire life. Then, it hit him one day that their underestimating him; it had nothing to do with him. It had to do with their choice to be judgmental versus being curious.

As leaders, we have the influence and authority to transform "us versus them" into environments where **we** can all thrive.

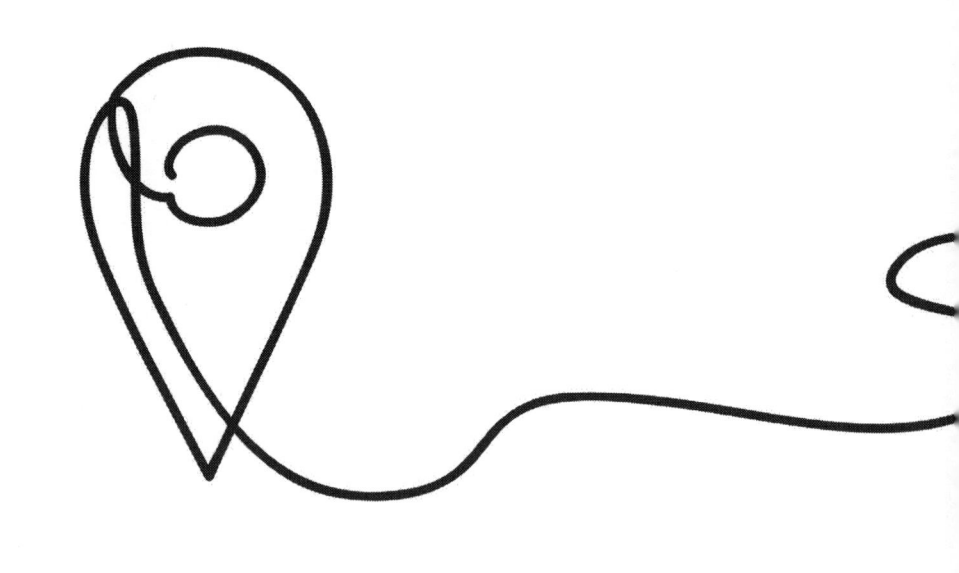

Chapter 8
THE NEXT STEPS

Well, friend. This concludes our coaching conversation, at least for now. I hope our time together sparked some insights that will serve you well. As adults, when we're exposed to new information, it's vital that we reflect on how we will apply it to our lives; otherwise, we'll forget and squander the progress we've made.

Although you may have gained several ideas that you'd like to act upon, I suggest prioritizing only the ones with the highest propensity to help you and your team thrive.

List the top three ideas or concepts that resonate the most based on everything we've discussed.

Help Them Thrive

1. _____

2. _____

3. _____

Action Planning

Starting with the end in mind helps us break down action plans into feasible steps and mitigates inaction or feeling overwhelmed. So, let's imagine we're chatting one year

The Next Steps

from now and celebrating how well you've evolved as a leader. What steps did you take, and by when?

Today's date is_____.

Milestone Date	Steps I took to help them and myself thrive.
One week from today.	
30 days from today.	
90 days from today.	
Six months from today.	
One year from today.	

How did you measure your success?

_____
_____
_____
_____
_____

Help Them Thrive

What risks did you encounter and how did you mitigate them?

Who did you turn to for guidance and support?

What did you do to sustain your momentum?

In closing, I want you to know that I believe in you. The fact that you're reading this book is evidence of your choice to **help them thrive**. Serving as your coach has been an honor.

I have a gift for you — access to the Help Them Thrive Readers page. Scan this QR code to unlock helpful resources and to keep our coaching conversation going.

Your friend, with coaching benefits,

Melissa

ACKNOWLEDGMENTS

In the journey of bringing this book to life, I have been blessed with the unwavering support and inspiration of incredible individuals who have played pivotal roles in my life. Their contributions have been immeasurable, and I want to express my heartfelt gratitude to each one of them.

First and foremost, to my loving husband, Terrance, whose endless support, patience, and good cooking, were my fuel throughout this writing process. I am endlessly grateful for your presence in my life.

To my two sweet kids, Little Terrance and Luke, you

both bring boundless joy and inspiration to my days. Your laughter and love have been my constant motivation, reminding me of the importance of the stories we share and the impact they can have on generations to come.

A special mention goes to my Uncle Scotty, my informal life coach, whose wisdom and guidance have been invaluable. Your insights have been a guiding light, shaping not only this book but also my journey toward personal growth and fulfillment.

I extend my deepest appreciation to my life coach, Lee Papa (leepapa.com), whose transformative guidance helped me, at a God-appointed time, to navigate the complexities of this writing journey and find inner peace in my life. Your wisdom and support have been instrumental in shaping my own self-discovery and confidence.

Aisha Houston, my niece, friend, life-saving assistant, and greatest encourager. Your dedication and partnership have been a blessing, and I am grateful to have you as an essential part of my journey.

I would also like to express my thanks to my speaker management team Michele Lucia and Canesha Appleton, with ADL Speakers, for their unwavering belief in me and their advocacy for my work. Thank you for helping me thrive.

Acknowledgments

To TEDx Speaker Stacy White, you are my Memento Mori Muse. Thank you for including me in your journey and awakening me to this powerful life concept. I am a better person for knowing you.

To my clients, who make me feel like I am living my life's purpose and making a difference in this world, I extend my deepest gratitude. Your trust and collaboration inspire me to continue pursuing meaningful work. I would not have a business without you. Thank you!

To my Aunties Julie and Marcie, you've made me look good my entire life. From instilling a much-needed fashion sense at an early age to proofing and editing this book, your guidance has played a significant role in shaping me into a better person.

A big shout-out goes to my brother Shawn and sister-in-law, Ashleigh for your embodiment of adventure and a relentless pursuit of a fulfilled life. Your boundless enthusiasm, courage, and zest for exploration have been a constant source of inspiration throughout this journey.

In every twist and turn of life's adventure, you have shown me the beauty of embracing challenges and seeking fulfillment in every moment. Your fearless pursuit of a life well-lived has been a guiding light, encouraging me to step out of my comfort zone and embrace the exhilarating unknown.

Help Them Thrive

A special acknowledgment goes to my parents, the unwavering pillars of strength, and the wind beneath my wings. You are the ones who taught me to dream fearlessly and reach for the stars. Your love has been a sanctuary in times of challenge. This book is as much a reflection of your influence as it is of my own endeavors.

In profound humility, I extend my deepest gratitude to God, the source of all inspiration and the force behind this creative endeavor. Throughout the twists and turns of this writing journey, I have felt the presence of divine grace, providing strength, clarity, and a calm sense of purpose.

Finally, I want to thank myself. Amid challenges and triumphs, I granted myself grace and permission to be authentically human. This journey has been a testament to the power of perseverance, self-awareness, and belief, and I am proud to have embraced my own authenticity and vulnerability in the process.

To all who have been a part of this incredible journey, thank you for your unwavering support, belief, and love. This book is not just mine; it is a collective achievement made possible by the strength of our shared connections and experiences.

Cheers to thriving!

Acknowledgments

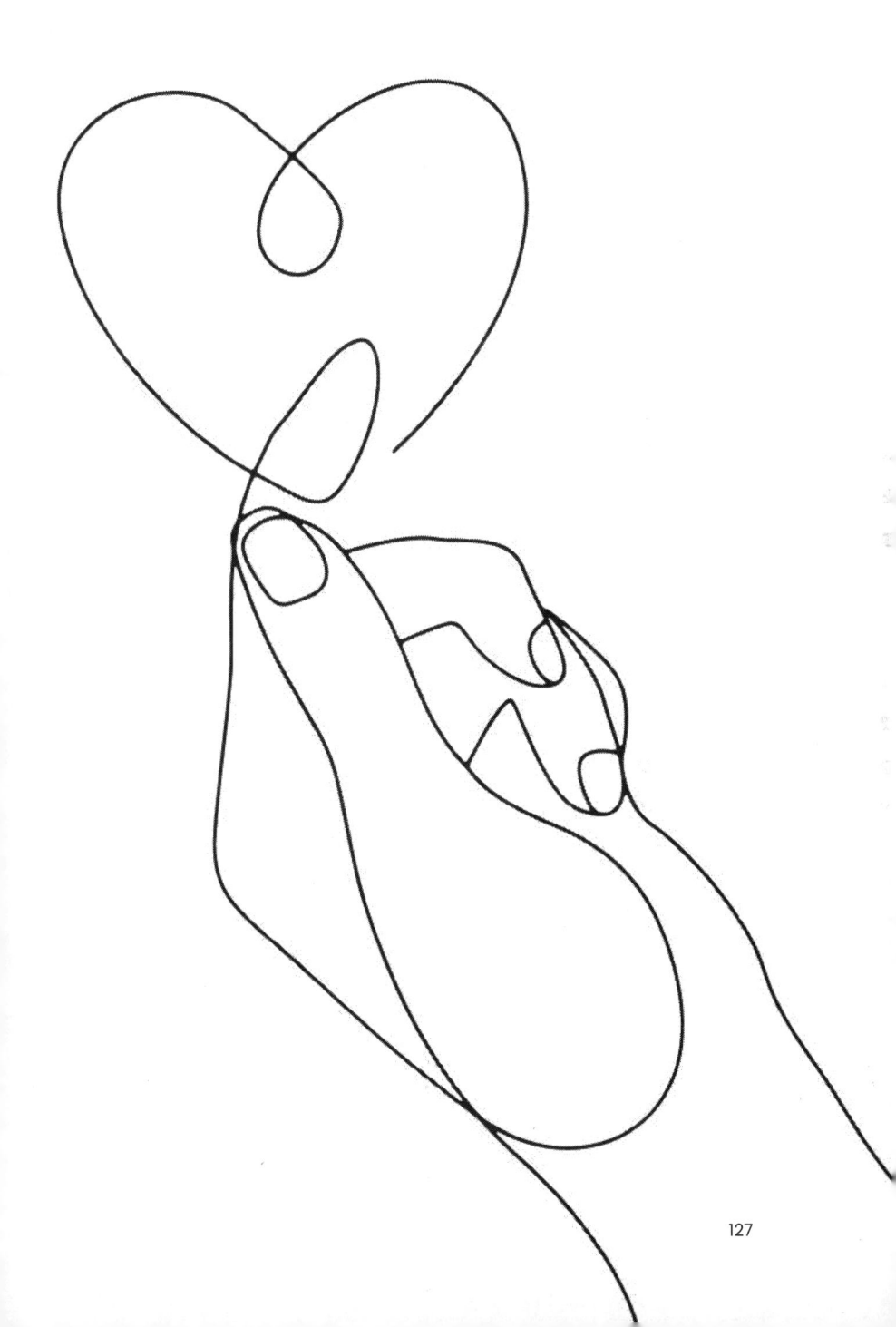

About The Author

Melissa Majors is a highly sought-after coach and speaker who is known for delivering engaging, brain-friendly and fun learning experiences that inspire people to take action.

She is the author of Help Them Thrive, The 7 Simple Habits of Inclusive Leaders and the founder of Melissa Majors Consulting, which provides a range of resources to help clients become better leaders.

Melissa is an expert in human-centered leadership practices that improve profitability, drive innovation, and enhance the employee experience. She studied strategy and innovation at Harvard University and has shared her insights through articles in Forbes, The Meeting Professional, and other publications, as well as on keynote speeches for organizations like the National Association of Realtors, 7-Eleven, RTX (formerly Raytheon), 1440 Multiversity, Catalyst and many more.

Despite her many accomplishments, Melissa remains down-to-earth and authentic and is passionate about helping people thrive in all areas of their lives.

To learn more about Melissa Majors and her work, please visit her website at melissamajors.com.

Made in the USA
Columbia, SC
24 November 2024